Writing an  Research Paper

A Roadmap for Beginning and Experienced Writers

PRESTWICK HOUSE, INC.

"Everything for the English Classroom!"

Writers:
Douglas Grudzina and Boris Kolba

Senior Editor:
Paul Moliken

Cover and Text Design:
Maria J. Mendoza

Layout and Production:
Jerry Clark

PRESTWICK HOUSE, INC.
"Everything for the English Classroom!"

P.O. Box 658

Clayton • Delaware 19938

Tel: 1.888.932.4593

Fax: 1.888.718.9333

Web: www.prestwickhouse.com

Printed in the United States of America. Revised, 2010

ISBN: 978-1-60389-013-7

Writing an A⁺ Research Paper

Research Paper

A Roadmap for Beginning and Experienced Writers

By Douglas Grudzina
& Boris Kolba

PRESTWICK HOUSE, INC.
"Everything for the English Classroom!"

Table of Contents

HOW IS THIS BOOK DIFFERENT FROM ALL OTHER BOOKS?

To be assigned a research paper is probably one of the most stressful events in the life of a high school student, but it does not need to be, because, as this book will show you, a research paper is really nothing more than a well-written essay that contains information from sources other than your own mind.

The mystique of the research paper lies essentially in the time allowed a student to write one and in the arcane system of citation, documentation, and attribution that make a research paper *look like* a research paper. Stripped of its trappings, however, the research assignment is not terribly different from any other writing assignment. In fact, it should be a pleasant time for you to learn more about something that really interests you and then show off your knowledge to your teacher.

Most other research paper guides and handbooks perpetuate the "cult of the difficult task" by focusing on the form and format and dividing the task into smaller chores, each of which is made to look insurmountable in its own way. Those research guides provide a few models and then leave you stranded just as you are about to begin your own paper in earnest.

This book won't.

Writing an A+ Research Paper will stay with you from the first day of school to the day you turn in your final draft. More than that even, this book will provide you with companionship as you embark on this rite of passage. As you work on your research project, you will meet Ella and Rob, who also have been assigned research papers. Ella will be your model, and you will actually be asked to help Rob. Then, you'll have the opportunity to apply what you've learned and practiced to your own research assignment. Your teacher might also ask you to help some other students, Eva, Ian, and Nikki, as they navigate the waters of the research pool.

Follow the steps in this book. Look at what your five companions have done. Practice with the included exercises, and most of all…enjoy. Your confidence will build as your understanding of the process increases. In addition, you'll probably find yourself enjoying the search, since the veil of the *unknown* and *unknowable* has been lifted.

The assignment of a research paper will no longer be a moment of dread, but an opportunity to explore.

One important thing you need to know is that, in this book's samples and exercises, we've made up just about all of the sources and most of the facts. It is, therefore, in your best interest *not to cite any of the sources or information in this book if you ever do a research paper on any of the topics developed here.*

You should do your own research anyway. That's what this book is about.

Okay…let's begin.

Chapter
1

COMING TO TERMS

It is the first day of the school year. You're catching up with old friends, meeting some new ones, and starting brand new classes. Each teacher tells you a bit about the work you will be doing in the year ahead. All of your classes sound interesting, and some even sound like they could be fun. Then, one of your teachers announces that over the months ahead, you will be writing a **research paper**.

If you're like many students, those words stop you in your tracks.

You've probably done some form of research before, at least an encyclopedia report on the Pilgrims in the fourth grade, and you almost certainly will be doing research in the future, in virtually every academic class you take through high school and college and graduate school—if you choose to go that far. Research is unavoidable. Still, the fact remains that **most students simply do not understand *the purpose* of the research paper assignment and, therefore, how to fulfill that purpose**.

This book will help you solve that problem. In the chapters ahead, we'll cover every aspect of researching and writing your research paper. We'll also follow the progress of several students writing their research papers, from choosing a topic, through doing the research and developing a thesis, to outlining, drafting and revising the final paper. You'll even get to help some of these students with their papers and practice everything you're learning. Then, you'll apply it to your own research assignment.

In this chapter, we'll start at the logical beginning, with the definition of what a research paper actually is.

1. What is a research paper?

As we said, the phrase "research paper" is probably not new to you—and neither are similar phrases like "research report" and "research project." But do all of those phrases mean the same thing? If not, how are they different?

Take a few minutes and write a few sentences explaining what you believe a research paper is. If you find it helpful to explain the research paper by comparing it to a "report" or a "project," go ahead.

Your explanation might read something like this: "A research paper is a paper that uses quotations from sources…and has a bibliography or something like that." If you offered an explanation anything like this, you are not completely wrong, but you certainly do not yet have a clear enough understanding to write that A+ paper. Let's begin with a short and sweet definition of what it is your teacher wants you to write:

A research paper is a thesis-driven essay that uses relevant, credible sources to support its ideas and arguments.

Now, let's examine each part of the definition.

> **A thesis-driven essay**: An *essay* is a relatively short piece of writing (compared to, say, a dissertation or a book) that *gives the author's point of view on a subject.*

A *thesis* is the main idea or argument of an essay.

No doubt, you've heard both of these terms before, but it's important to remember just what they mean. An essay does more than just explain what its subject is; it tells what you, as the author, think about the subject. A *thesis-driven essay*, therefore, focuses on its thesis. The entire essay presents, develops, and supports that main idea or argument.

For more on your thesis, turn to "**What is a thesis?**" on pages 19-21.

> **Relevant, credible sources**: A *source* is anything or anyone that gives you information and ideas. Finding and studying sources is the *research* part of writing a research paper. Sources can include books, encyclopedias, newspapers, magazines, websites, and interviews with knowledgeable people. Before you write your research paper, your sources will tell you what you need to know about your topic; and in the paper itself, they will support your ideas, giving weight to your point of view. Does that sound like a lot to expect from your sources? It is a lot, which is why your sources must be *relevant* and *credible*. A source is *relevant* if it presents information that will be useful to you. A source is *credible* if it is trustworthy, and if the information in it is accurate and up-to-date.

⌐ For more on sources, turn to "**What Are 'Relevant' and 'Credible' Sources?**" on pages 60-87.

> **Support its ideas and arguments**: This is the kind of phrase most students ignore. You've been told many, many times to "support your ideas and arguments" so it's easy to treat this part of the definition as mere filler, but it is *very* important. This phrase tells you something crucial about the relationship between your thesis and your research. In a research paper, your thesis is the most important element. Your sources are there *only to support your thesis*. Never forget this! You can have the best sources in the world, but without a strong thesis, you do *not* have a research paper! By the same token, you can have the most brilliant thesis ever developed, but if you do not have concrete information from valid sources, you do not have a research paper.

Let's pause now and look at a few students and some work they've been doing. Read the descriptions of their projects and then decide whether each project meets our definition of a research paper—and why.

EXERCISE ONE:

DETERMINING WHAT A RESEARCH PAPER IS

Complete the following explanation

Rob, to whom you were introduced earlier, is learning about the American Civil War in his social studies class. Outside of class, he's read two books written by well-known historians about the battle of Gettysburg. He's also read three articles that his teacher has recommended on the same subject. Then, he writes a paper that explains the main points of each of the books and articles he's read.

This paper IS NOT a research paper because . . .

We are going to follow Rob and Ella as they follow the process and write the research paper their teacher is assigning today. (Your teacher my also want you to work with their classmates Eva, Ian, and Nikki.) Let's look at the assignment they are given on the first day of classes of the spring semester:

ROB AND ELLA'S RESEARCH PAPER ASSIGNMENT

Write a research paper on an important issue in early United States history. Choose one of the following topics:

- Colonial New England
- Colonial Jamestown
- Slavery in the Colonies
- The Revolutionary War
- The Constitutional Convention
- Westward Expansion

These are very, very __broad__ topics. No matter which one you choose, you'll need to make your topic more manageable.

For more on narrowing a topic, see pages 28–33.

Focus on one aspect of your topic. You may focus on a single problem, what caused that problem, and how it was solved (or not solved). For example, if you chose the Constitutional Convention, you could focus on **the question of slavery and how it was addressed in the Constitution.**

You could also focus on one event, what led to it, and its long-term effects. For example, if you chose the topic of Westward Expansion, you could focus on the Louisiana Purchase, including **what led up to it** and **how it affected America's growth and development.**

Statements like these could be the beginning of a thesis.

For more on coming up with a preliminary thesis, see pages 19–21.

REQUIREMENTS

- 6–10 typed pages, double-spaced, front of page only

- At least five sources
  - What kinds of sources will you need? Where will you find them? Does five seem like a lot?
  For more on sources, see Chapter 3.

- MLA-style citations and Works Cited Page
  - What does this mean? MLA style is one of the special formal requirements for research papers.
  For more on citations and Works Cited Pages, see pages 196-201.

NOTE: **Plagiarism will result in an automatic failing grade!**
A failing grade for plagiarism? That's serious! We'll talk about plagiarism and how you can avoid it throughout the book. For now, all you need to know is that *every time you use information from a source, you must give that source appropriate credit, or you are committing plagiarism.*

DEADLINES

- Monday, April 14th
  Topic
- Monday, May 5th
  Preliminary list of sources
- Tuesday, May 27th
  Rough draft
- Friday, June 10th
  Final draft

Chapter 2 covers choosing a topic. Chapters 3 and 4 are on finding sources. Chapter 6 covers writing your rough draft. Chapter 7 deals with writing your final draft.

EXERCISE TWO:

REVIEWING IMPORTANT DEFINITIONS

Write a brief definition for each of the following terms.

Thesis

Source

Relevant and credible

Plagiarism

2. What is research?

It almost goes without saying that research is an essential part of a "research paper." It's what distinguishes a research paper from any other kind of essay. You can eloquently express your opinion on a topic, but without research, your opinion is all you have. You have a right to your opinion, but that right does not obligate anyone to agree with you. Research, however, greatly increases the likelihood that your reader will agree with your thesis. At the very least, research provides you with the support and details that establish your thesis as valid and make your reader consider your point, even if he or she does not agree with it completely.

But what exactly is research?

The dictionary defines *research* as "investigating or studying a topic closely and thoroughly." You probably do research more often than you realize. Have you ever searched the Internet for information about a new game console you want to buy? That's research. Have you ever read two or three reviews of a movie you might want to see? That's research, too.

Basically, **research is the act of learning about a topic independently, using sources of information beyond classroom materials**.

What does this tell you? Here are a few important points to remember:

> **Research is a way to learn about a topic.** Research is more than just collecting quotations for your paper. It's one of the best ways you can learn. The more information you take in, the more you will know about your topic. In fact, when you do research, you become an "expert" on your topic!

For more on learning from your sources, turn to "**What do I do with all of these sources?**" on page 139.

> **Research is something you do outside the classroom.** You've probably already learned at least a little about your topic in class. When you do research, however, you move beyond the classroom—into the library, onto the Internet, and even into the

community. In that way, you learn more about your topic than you can in class alone.

⌂ For more on where to do research, turn to "**Where can I find the sources I need?**" on pages 88-99.

> **Research is something you do independently.** Your teacher might provide some help by recommending a source or suggesting where you should look. You, however, will do the bulk of your research—finding information and learning from it—on your own.

The process of research can actually be divided into two basic stages. **Stage one** is *gathering information about your topic.* You sit at your computer, punching keywords into search engines. You hunt through online and print magazines for articles about your topic. Maybe you travel to the library, looking for additional print sources, especially books. You might even track down an expert on your topic whom you can interview, either in person, on the telephone, or via e-mail or electronic chat. Any of these can be **sources** for your research paper.

⌂ For more on types of sources, turn to "**What are sources?**" on pages 43-59.

Gathering ample sources is obviously crucial—and remember that, at some point, you will have to evaluate those sources for relevance and credibility—but it's not the whole story. **Stage two** of research is *learning from the information you've gathered.* Remember, research is a way to learn about a topic. You'll likely find more than enough potential sources on any topic you choose to write about, but having the sources and taking random information from each will not result in your learning very much or being able to put together a very useful research paper. Part of our definition of research, then, is that it has to be **organized**. The search itself has to be organized, and the end product—the paper—has to be organized.

When you know what you want to learn from your sources, and you give some earnest thought to what you'd like to teach your reader, you'll be able to make the most of your research.

The best research papers do not merely discuss the information, they also discuss the sources, explaining how the thesis developed and where the paper-writer's ideas came from.

◁ For more on learning from your research, turn to "**What do I do with all of these sources?**" on page 139.

3. What is a thesis?

Thesis is another word you've no doubt heard and used a number of times before. It can mean something general, such as "the most important part of an essay," or it might zero in on something as specific as "the last sentence of an essay's first paragraph." Neither definition does much to help you understand exactly what a thesis actually is.

The dictionary definition of *thesis* is "a proposition supported by an argument." Any time you make an argument, you have a thesis. If you try to convince your parents that your curfew is unreasonably early, your thesis could be: "I should be allowed to stay out later on weekends." If you're telling skeptical friends just how amazing a feat it is to win the Tour de France seven times, your thesis is probably: "Lance Armstrong is a great athlete." In both cases, your thesis is the actual point you are arguing.

For a research paper, we can define a thesis this way:

A thesis is the central argument about a topic, supported by facts, ideas, and examples collected through research.

You already know that a research paper is *thesis-driven*. It does more than merely report what you've learned about your topic—it makes a case about your topic. The thesis is at the core, and the whole paper focuses on making and supporting that argument. Of course, almost every essay you write for school has a thesis, but a research paper thesis is different, for a couple of reasons:

> **A research paper thesis is based on your research.**
> Remember, research is a way you learn about your topic. Your thesis—the argument you make about your topic—must be based on what you learn. You can think about your thesis from the beginning, but your research comes first—your final thesis will grow out of that research.

> **A research paper thesis is supported by your research.**
> Trying to explain the relationship between your thesis and your research (your thesis grows out of your research, and your research is governed by your thesis) is something like the chicken-or-the-egg puzzle.

Still, your paper must be driven by your thesis—your research is there *only* to show that your argument is valid. You need to use the information that supports your thesis in your paper, and leave out the information that isn't related to your argument.

◿ For more on using your thesis to choose sources, turn to "**How should I use sources in my paper?**" on pages 184-186.

Remembering that your thesis is supposed to be an argument and that your paper is the demonstration of that argument's validity will help us establish a few more important points in our definition:

> **Your thesis should not look like your topic.** Suppose your topic is slavery in the American colonies, and you come up with this thesis: *Slavery played a major role in the American colonies.* This is much too close to the topic itself. If you simply restate the topic, you aren't really making an argument—and your thesis needs to be an argument. A statement like: *When New England states abolished slavery, it was more for economic reasons than for moral ones,* makes a much better thesis.

> **Your thesis should not be too "big."** Your thesis needs to be complex enough to drive your research paper, but a thesis can end up being *too* big and complex for the assignment. Remember that you are writing a 6-10-page paper, not a book. A thesis on slavery in the American colonies could read: *Slavery shaped the American colonies in ways that can still be seen today,* but you'd need a whole book to make this argument in any real depth. It will be better to offer a narrower, more manageable argument: *The reasons New England states abolished slavery much earlier than Southern states had more to do with their economy than their moral consciences.*

> **Your thesis should not be too "small."** If your thesis is too narrow and specific, however, it won't be able to sustain an entire research paper. Consider again the paper on slavery in the colonies. This time, you're careful not to make your thesis too big: *Between 1700 and 1750, slavery in Virginia quadrupled.* This thesis goes too far in the other direction. It's not a big enough argument to fill 6-10 pages—it's too narrow. However, there's another big problem with this thesis, as well.

> **Your thesis must be an argument.** The "thesis" offered above: *Between 1700 and 1750, slavery in Virginia quadrupled,* is either true or it isn't. Granted, you might not *know* whether it's true, and you'd have to do some research to verify whether that is an accurate statistic or not, but all you would be doing is *verifying a fact,* not arguing a thesis. An argument involving the increase of slavery in Virginia might read: *Without the enormous increase in the number of slaves from 1700 to 1750, Virginia would not have reached the economic and political prominence it enjoyed in the early days of the United States.*

Taking into consideration the previous four points, then, your thesis needs to be an argument that will comfortably fill 6-10 pages, and can be supported with information from five (or more) sources.

⌂ For more on developing your thesis, turn to "**How do I start thinking about a thesis?**" on pages 34-39 and "**How do I begin refining my thesis and outline?**" on pages 169-172.

4. What *isn't* a research paper?

By now, you should know what a research paper is: *a thesis-driven essay that uses relevant, credible sources to support its ideas and arguments.* You know what research and credible, relevant sources are. You know what a research paper thesis is, as well.

It follows, then, that there are a few things a research paper is *not*, and understanding them will certainly help you turn in that A+ paper.

> A research paper isn't **a report**. Perhaps the most common misconception about research papers is that the paper simply presents what you learned from your research.

   Always remember that the research paper is thesis-driven, that every bit of information presented from every source consulted is governed by the central argument that *you devised*. In your paper, you will be comparing, contrasting, interpreting, and evaluating the information you present, all with an eye toward establishing the validity of *your* thesis, *your* argument.

> A research paper isn't **cutting and pasting**. Research is a learning process. You learn by examining the work of experts who know your topic. You might think that your sources capture your topic in words much more effectively than you can. It might be really tempting to let them do the talking for you, by cutting and pasting big blocks of text from your sources into your paper. Aside from ethical issues and the illegality of plagiarism, which we will discuss in great length later, this method of creating a paper will certainly give you a product to turn in, but you will not have learned a thing about your topic. Remember that the focus of your research paper is *your thesis*—your sources play only a supporting role.

> A research paper isn't a **glitzy presentation**. Some students spend a great deal of time on charts, graphics, impressive headings, and fancy fonts—more time, in fact, than they put into their research or their theses. These students end up very disappointed with low grades that don't seem to reflect the time they spent.

Remember that your research paper is a *thesis-driven essay*. Your thesis and your research—and how you bring them together—are what matter. "Artistic" use of fonts, graphics, and the like do not. Time you spend working on these kinds of production values is largely wasted.

> A research paper isn't a **picture book**. So far, we've talked about researching ideas and information. When you do research, though, you may also find *images*. If you're looking into the Revolutionary War, you might find etchings of famous battles, or you might come across maps from the early 1800s as you examine westward expansion.

Images like these are fascinating, and they can help you visualize the issues you're researching. Students often want to clip the images they find and include them in their papers. At best, images distract you from making and supporting your argument. At worst, the images crowd out your thesis and other research. If four pages are filled up with images, you do not have a 6-10 page research paper.

Now, if you feel you *absolutely must* present a map or political cartoon, do so in an appendix at the end of your paper. Refer to the appendix in the body of your text, and *do not include the appendix page(s) in your ultimate page count*.

> A research paper isn't **a list of websites or other sources**. Certainly you'll refer to your sources, cite them, and include a Works Cited Page or bibliography (which, by the way, *does not* count toward your 6-10 pages), but the research paper is a type of *essay*. You have a lot of discussing to do, evaluating, interpreting, etc. If all you do is list your sources, you might as well not bother.

> A research paper isn't **a collection of quotations, paraphrases, or summaries**. As we've said, the research paper is an *essay*. Whatever you present from your sources is secondary, existing *only* to support your argument. Again, if all you do is compile notes, no matter how fancily you dress them up, you have not written a research paper.

Knowing what to avoid is your first step to that A+. Before we actually begin our project, let's look at what to do that will give you a top-graded paper.

5. What earns a research paper an A+?

We hope that it's already clearer what you need to produce and turn in to get an A+, but there are still some basic things you can do to nudge your paper's grade from C to B, from B to A, and from A to A+.

Your paper may be the longest in the class, with an extensive list of sources, but it still won't earn a top grade unless it has the following:

> **A strong thesis.** We can't stress this enough. If you do not have a thesis, if your thesis is too broad or too narrow, if your thesis is not really an argument or is an obvious argument, no matter how much else you do right, you will have, at best, a mediocre paper.

> **A range of relevant and credible sources.** Two pop-culture magazine articles and a blog do not constitute research. You want a really good grade? Do some good research, find some sources, and study them to learn something about your topic.

> **Good organization and writing.** The final draft of your research paper—the final draft of your thesis-driven essay—must be an example of your best writing. If you are careful with the process through which we'll guide you in this book, you won't have any problem organizing your information, but you have to be committed to a well-written and organized *essay* from the very beginning.

> **Correct use of source citation and attribution.** No one may be willing to admit this, but some part of your grade will be subjective—does your research paper *sound like* a research paper? We're not suggesting that a poorly researched paper with weak sources and faulty logic will get an A+ simply because it "sounds good," but it is possible that you can bump your grade from B to A, or A to A+ by paying attention to how you discuss your sources.

Being transparent about the sources you used and how you used them is absolutely essential to a top-graded research paper. You are, in a sense, not only explaining what you learned, but how you learned it as well.

- **A strong presence of original thought and insight.** Remember, you are not writing a report. Your thesis is supposed to be your argument, something you realized while examining your sources, and something you need to prove to your reader. If you turn in a compilation of what all your sources said instead of an actual research paper, you probably will not fail, but, most likely, you will not receive a grade higher than a C.

- **Proper formatting.** You will receive instructions on how to set up the paper—where to put your name, information about your course and teacher, due date, and other necessary details. You'll also receive instructions about how to set up your Works Cited Page, how to punctuate parenthetical citations, etc. Follow these instructions. Again, a poorly written but beautifully formatted paper will not receive an A just for its format, but a beautifully written paper that is not formatted according to the instructions can be returned without a grade.

Of course, you also want to avoid even the appearance of plagiarism, and we will discuss this in much greater detail later on. For now, let's pause, take a deep breath, and begin our research project.

Chapter
2

SEARCHERS, START YOUR ENGINES

In Chapter 1, we learned what a research paper is. We defined the most important terms—research, thesis, sources, and so on—and we talked about the steps in a research project. Now, it's time to start working on an actual research paper. Starting with this chapter, we'll go through the whole process, from start to finish.

Remember that research is a *process* of learning. If you try to take the whole assignment in a single gulp, it will prove to be intimidating, so instead of trying to do everything at once, we're going to take the research paper step by step. When your teacher assigns a research paper, those steps are usually built in. For example, the assignment we saw on page 8 broke everything down into steps, each one with a due date of its own. To keep up your pace and finish each step on time, follow the teacher's schedule.

In this chapter, we'll go through the beginning steps of the research paper process. We'll go back to the assignment itself. This time, however, instead of breaking it down and analyzing the pieces, we'll actually choose a topic and start narrowing it. Then, we'll get ready for the work ahead.

To illustrate how the research paper process really works, we'll follow a student named Ella as she works through her own research paper. We'll take a look at her thoughts as she chooses and narrows a topic, conducts research, comes up with a thesis, drafts her paper, revises, and so on. (She isn't here to do the work *for you*, of course, so don't plan to borrow her topic or notes!) Ella's progress will shed light on each step as you work on your own paper.

Since you can't accomplish anything until you choose and narrow your topic, that's the first step you'll need to take.

6. What is a good topic for a research paper?

Basically, your **topic** is the general subject of your research paper. When someone asks you what your research paper is "about," you'll answer with your topic. Naturally, the first step in any research paper project is choosing a topic and shaping it to match the assignment.

Your teacher will probably address the issue of topics in one of three ways:

> Sometimes, an assignment will ask you to **come up with a topic entirely on your own**, which may sound terrifying. If you're free to choose any topic under the sun, where on Earth should you start? Remember, however, that the assignment is part of a class that has a subject or "topic" of its own, such as United States history or English literature. Your teacher expects you to stick with that subject and to dig deeper into something you've covered in class.

> That still gives you a lot of freedom. What topic should you choose? Since you'll be working with this subject matter for a while to come, choose a topic you're interested in or curious about. It's also a good idea to choose a topic about which you already know at least a little. It's *very* difficult to know where to even *begin* researching a topic about which you know nothing. Remember that a "free-choice" topic is still supposed to be rooted in material covered in class.

> More often, the instructor will ask you to **choose from a few topics** that are provided. Obviously, assignments like these don't give you as much freedom, but they do make choosing a topic much easier. Even in this case, however, like the examples on page 12, the suggested topics will be broad and need to be narrowed down—personalized to suit your interest and curiosity.

> On occasion, your teacher will **assign one topic** and one topic only. With an assignment like this, there's no choosing for you to do. Does that mean you can skip this step altogether? No, it doesn't—you still have to shape that assigned topic and make it your own.

As the very first step of the research paper project, your teacher will probably require you to hand in your topic for approval. He or she will most likely offer your guidance on sufficiently narrowing the topic without narrowing it too much and developing a topic that will lend itself to an argument.

Ultimately, because an essay allows you to discuss *your view* on a topic, and the foundation of the research paper is the point *you* want to argue, this process of narrowing even an assigned topic allows you to make the final topic uniquely yours.

How does this narrowing and shaping work? To get a better picture, let's turn to Ella. Ella's history teacher has given her class the same assignment we saw on page 12. Let's take another look at the choice of topics:

ROB AND ELLA'S RESEARCH PAPER ASSIGNMENT

Write a research paper on an important issue in early United States history. Choose one of the following topics:

- Colonial New England
- Colonial Jamestown
- Slavery in the Colonies
- The Revolutionary War
- The Constitutional Convention
- Westward Expansion

Take a look at the choices—what do they have in common? They're all about early United States history, of course, and they're all *very broad*. Each of these could be the topic for a book (or series of books). That's why students are told they must "focus on one aspect of [their] topic." Ella knows that whatever she chooses, she'll have to narrow her topic down before she turns it in for approval.

Choosing, however, comes first, and Ella decides she likes "Colonial Jamestown" for her initial, very broad topic. The story of Jamestown interested Ella when her class covered it earlier in the school year. She'd like to learn more about Jamestown, and she's sure she'll stay interested throughout the research paper project. Now, it's time for her to narrow her topic down. Remember, Ella is not trying to write her thesis yet. That takes research, but before she goes any further, she needs to sharpen her focus and zero in on one specific aspect of the broad topic of Jamestown. A narrower topic will guide Ella's research and keep her from trying to cram an overly ambitious thesis into 6-10 pages.

Where does she start? Ella knows that Jamestown was the first successful English colony in North America, but what else does she know about it? What other information does she have on hand? First, Ella turns to the textbook her class is using. Here, she finds a general overview of that pioneering settlement that gives her food for thought.

Even at this early stage, Ella should get in the habit of keeping a record of the information she will eventually need for her Works Cited Page: author's name; title of article; title of book, magazine, newspaper, web site, etc.; URL for websites; date and city of publication for print sources; copyright date; page numbers; and so on. Right now, format is not important, but it will save Ella time later if she gathers this information now.

Let's take a look at Ella's textbook, and listen in to the ideas it gave her.

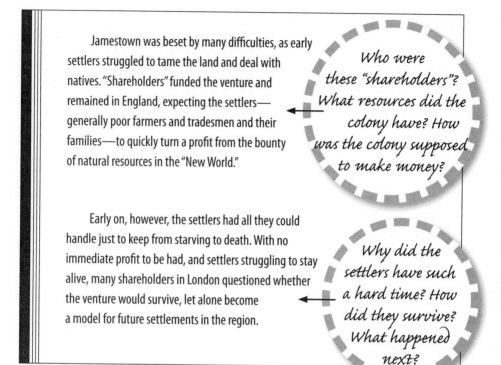

Jamestown was beset by many difficulties, as early settlers struggled to tame the land and deal with natives. "Shareholders" funded the venture and remained in England, expecting the settlers—generally poor farmers and tradesmen and their families—to quickly turn a profit from the bounty of natural resources in the "New World."

Who were these "shareholders"? What resources did the colony have? How was the colony supposed to make money?

Early on, however, the settlers had all they could handle just to keep from starving to death. With no immediate profit to be had, and settlers struggling to stay alive, many shareholders in London questioned whether the venture would survive, let alone become a model for future settlements in the region.

Why did the settlers have such a hard time? How did they survive? What happened next?

Reading in her textbook and thinking about what she learned in class begins a train of thought for Ella. Let's take a look at her notebook and see how she narrows her topic from broad to specific.

From Ella's Notes

- Colonial Jamestown: First successful English colony in America

- Successful = made a profit. No profit at first. Somehow settlers turned it around.

- Model for future settlements. How/why? What does "model" mean? That's why Jamestown was important—interesting!

- Research how Jamestown was a model for English settlements?

Soon, Ella has her focused, specific topic: Jamestown's role as a model for future English settlements in North America.

Ella reads on in her notes and in her textbook. She even starts doing a little bit of research on the Internet, searching to further develop her thoughts. Of course, she writes down her ideas in her notes. First, however, she turns in her topic to her teacher for approval. Once she gets that approval, her notes become the beginning of her thesis.

We'll talk about preliminary theses more in our next section, **"How do I start thinking about a thesis?"** on pages 34–39.

EXERCISE ONE:

PRACTICING NARROWING TOPICS

Rob, another student in Ella's class, could use some help narrowing his topic. Follow the process Ella used and advise Rob how to focus his topic by filling in the missing steps for him.

Rob's Topic

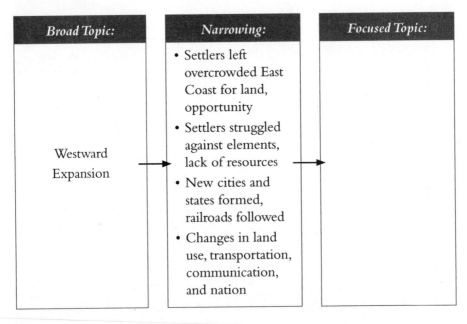

Broad Topic:	Narrowing:	Focused Topic:
Westward Expansion	• Settlers left overcrowded East Coast for land, opportunity • Settlers struggled against elements, lack of resources • New cities and states formed, railroads followed • Changes in land use, transportation, communication, and nation	

EXERCISE TWO:

NARROW YOUR OWN RESEARCH TOPIC

Now, apply to your own research assignment what you have learned and practiced.

Complete as many of the following steps as you need to arrive at a focused topic you will enjoy working with for an extended period of time.

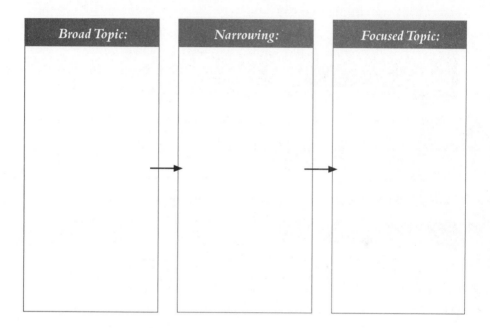

Broad Topic:	Narrowing:	Focused Topic:

7. How do I start thinking about a thesis?

You've turned in your topic, and your teacher has approved it. (Or perhaps you got some constructive criticism, made some changes, and then your teacher approved it.) Now, it's time to start thinking about the research paper itself, and the thesis that will drive it.

In Chapter 1, we defined a research paper thesis as **"the central argument about a topic, supported by facts, ideas, examples, and research."** Because a thesis is based on research, you're not ready to commit to one at this point in the game. However, we also learned that a research paper is *thesis-driven*—that is, the whole paper focuses on making and supporting that central argument. Therefore, even though you're not ready for a thesis yet, you need *something* to give direction to the planning of your paper.

What you need is a **preliminary thesis**. A preliminary thesis is like a first draft of your thesis. Your research will be directed by your preliminary thesis, and as you learn more and gather support, you'll refine it. You might even discover that your preliminary thesis won't work, and you have to develop a new one—this is not a bad thing since the research process is supposed to be a *learning* process. Think of this step as starting to ask the question that your research paper will answer.

A preliminary thesis comes *before* you dive into your research. However, it is natural—and helpful—to do some light reading about your topic at this stage. Type some key words into an Internet search engine and see what turns up. Read to see what interesting angles your topic might present that could be the seeds of a thesis. Jot down a few notes, but don't go into great detail.

⌁ For more about note-taking and research, turn to **"How do I take notes on my sources?"** on pages 140-151.)

You might end up not using any of these sources in your final paper, but be sure to record the necessary information for the Works Cited Page of your paper, just in case you *do* use some of this information. Your goal now is simply to get some background knowledge and develop your own perspective. It will help you build a preliminary thesis from your topic.

For example, Ella's broad topic was the Jamestown settlement. The focused topic she developed is *Jamestown's role as a model for future English settlements in North America*. As she continues to look through her textbook, notes, and a few Internet sources, she finds that the Jamestown settlement began to thrive only after the settlers were granted a certain degree of independence, and they started to grow tobacco as a cash crop in which they all had a vested interest. Ella tentatively drafts a **preliminary thesis:** *Changes in the management of the Jamestown settlement helped define the nature of future British colonies in North America—and eventually the United States.*

What makes this a good preliminary thesis? First, it's still broad in focus. To try to list *all* the lessons learned and argue how each led to the thirteen colonies that eventually became the United States would fill a book—and has, many times over. This broadness will give Ella some elbow room as she works, but it is also a real argument, a stand on her topic that requires information to back it up. In other words, it's a starting point for her research, which will help her develop the argument and refine her thesis.

⌁ For more on your research thesis, turn to **"How do I begin refining my thesis and outline?"** on pages 169-171.

But first, let's take a closer look at how Ella develops her preliminary thesis.

While looking through articles on the Internet, Ella reads something that catches her imagination:

The Virginia Company, Jamestown's financial backers, dreamed of endless New World bounty just waiting to be plucked. After all, their three-point mandate to the first settlers was to settle Virginia, to find gold, and discover a water route to the Far East. They were sorely disappointed by the lack of progress (i.e., profit) in the early years. They pressed company officers to push settlers to produce more, faster. However, the settlers did not appreciate the added pressures as they dealt with hunger, disease, pests, climate, and self-defense. They pushed back.

Eventually, changes in the basic economic and social structure of the settlement began to take hold. The communal work system under which the colony had been founded resulted only in poor production and starvation. Production, and therefore profit, increased only after the governor—against the wishes of his shareholders—assigned three-acre lots to the surviving original settlers to be farmed as their own private property. Smaller lots were granted to new arrivals.

That looks like a big idea! What does it mean?

This shift from a communal to a privatized economic structure radically altered Jamestown and led to a new mentality. Subsequent colonies would not be tenant-farmed plantations (as English colonies in other lands continued to be) but communities of pioneering, innovative, self-reliant, *land-owning* individuals... in other words, the future United States.

As you can see, Ella is struck by that last sentence. It seems the writer is saying that something about Jamestown played a key part in actually turning a handful of colonies into the United States. Ella wants to learn more. This could be the start of her thesis! She opens up her notebook and writes:

From Ella's Notes

- *Harsh conditions at Jamestown!!!*

- *Reasons for poor production in the beginning*

- *Reasons for improved production later on*

- *Changed relationship: settlers, bosses, share-holders*

- *Changes affected future of (English) colonies*

Ella knows she needs to find out more about how Jamestown changed, and how the changes helped shape the future development of the United States. Her research will help her figure out which questions to ask, and how to answer them. She also knows she needs to find sources she can use in her research paper.

◁ For more on making sure your sources measure up, turn to **"What are 'Relevant' and 'Credible' Sources?"** on pages 60-87.

Furthermore, Ella knows where to start her research. She has the beginning of an argument to make. She writes her preliminary thesis in her notes: Changes in the management of the Jamestown settlement helped define the nature of future British colonies in North America—and eventually the United States.

EXERCISE THREE:

PRACTICING WITH PRELIMINARY THESES

In Exercise One, you helped Rob narrow his assigned topics. Now, help him draft his preliminary thesis.

Rob's Topic

Broad Topic:	*Focused Topic:*	*Preliminary Thesis:*
Westward Expansion	How the development of the railroads increased the movement west and changed the nature of those who went.	

From Rob's history textbook:

The first Transcontinental Railroad in the United States, largely motivated by a desire to bind the Union together during the Civil War, was officially completed in the historic "golden spike" ceremony at Promontory Summit, Utah, on May 10, 1869. This railroad, which linked the already-thriving eastern railway network with California and the Pacific Ocean, would forever alter the population and economy of the West. The wagon trains of previous decades became obsolete overnight, and many say that the West was opened to a new breed of softer, greedier pioneer. This new, modern transportation system substantially increased the migration of white homesteaders and exacerbated the decline of Native Americans in these regions.

EXERCISE FOUR:

WRITING YOUR OWN THESIS

Now, apply to your own research assignment what you have learned and practiced.

Carefully consider your broad topic and your focused topic. Review your class notes, and look at your textbook. Take notes on what you read.

Then, draft a **preliminary thesis**.

Remember that this preliminary thesis will probably be refined as you continue to research—your research might even indicate that this thesis needs to be abandoned altogether—but it will give you an early guide for your reading and note taking.

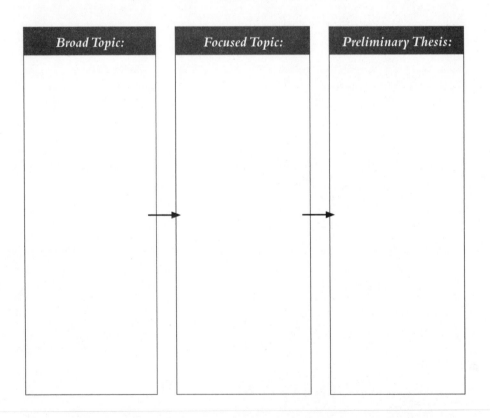

Broad Topic:	*Focused Topic:*	*Preliminary Thesis:*

8. What are the steps of the research process?

It's easy to understand why many students feel a bit intimidated at this point. Like a hiker at the base of a mountain, you know you have to climb to the top, and the path ahead looks awfully long and steep.

The truth is, however, that the path ahead may be long, but it doesn't have to be steep. A research paper process is nothing more than a series of manageable steps. By pacing yourself and taking each step as it comes, you'll get to the top of the mountain in great shape. So, before we take the next step, let's examine the road ahead. What will we be doing over the next few weeks?

The first two steps you've already accomplished. They are:

✔ Selecting and focusing your subject
✔ Developing a preliminary thesis

The remaining steps, which will fill the coming weeks, are:

> **Collecting Sources:** As we learned in Chapter 1, **a research paper is a thesis-driven essay that uses relevant, credible sources to support its ideas and arguments**, so clearly, you're going to need some "credible, relevant sources."

Collecting sources will be one of the longest stages of your research process; it will be the focus of Chapter 3.

> **Organizing Your Sources:** A week or two from now, once you have a stack of books on your floor, file folders full of magazine article reprints and photocopies, and two dozen web sites bookmarked on your computer, you'll probably be tempted to step back in panic and wonder what you're supposed to do with everything you have collected. What do you read first? How do you keep track of what concepts and information you get and from which sources they came so you don't end up being accused of plagiarism.

Keeping track of your sources and information will be another long stage and will be the focus of Chapter 4.

> **Finalizing Your Thesis:** Remember that your final research paper is to be a **thesis-driven essay.** Without a strong thesis, no matter how many sources you consult or what information you present, you will not have a research paper.

Developing your unique thesis and presenting your researched information in support of that thesis are also *very* effective ways to avoid charges of plagiarism.

Finalizing your thesis is the focus of Chapter 5.

> **Outlining:** Outlining is quite possibly the single best strategy for writing a successful essay. You've no doubt written outlines before, but there are special considerations when your outline includes research. We'll cover those considerations and create a research outline in Chapter 5, right after you finalize your thesis.

> **Drafting:** With a strong thesis, ample and organized notes, and a good outline, you can actually write the first draft of your 6–10 page paper in a few hours.

Chapter 6 focuses on writing the first draft of your research paper. The heart of this chapter will be Ella's complete first draft.

> **Finalizing Your Paper:** Your first draft is not the end of the road—that's why it's called a *first* draft! You may be required to turn your first draft in to your teacher, like Ella, and you will likely get it back with constructive criticism.

In Chapter 7, you'll learn how to edit and revise that first draft and compose the final draft of your research paper. We'll cover what makes a research paper complete and ready to hand in for a grade, and what makes a final draft so different from a first draft. You'll learn how to cite your sources properly and to protect yourself thoroughly from plagiarism.

All right, let's turn the page to Chapter 3 and begin.

THE HUNT IS ON

In Chapter 1, we defined research as "the act of learning about a topic independently, using sources of information beyond classroom materials." The work you've done so far toward that end has been fairly light treading. You've done some general reading on your topic and formed your first ideas. With these ideas to guide you, you're ready to make a serious investment of time and effort. Like the prosecutor in a criminal trial, it's your responsibility to make your case and support your ideas with serious research.

Now, it's time to begin that serious research.

9. What are sources?

A source is anything that gives you information or ideas. Many, many forms of information can be sources for researchers. Books, encyclopedias, newspapers, documentaries, magazines, CD-ROMs, databases, websites, interviews with knowledgeable people—all of these media. The information is usually more important than how it's communicated—especially today, when new media are emerging and old media are falling out of use.

Not all sources are equal, however, just as not all of the information they contain is equally useful. Distinguishing among sources is an essential part of research. In this section, we'll look at the most important kinds of sources, starting with the biggest categories of all: primary and secondary sources. No doubt you've heard these terms before. Your teacher may even require you to use primary sources—but what do they mean?

> A **primary source** is an original work that gives you firsthand information about your topic. Primary sources have a *direct relationship* to your topic, whether the subject is an historical event, a famous person, a significant idea, or whatever. The exact relationship between a primary source and your topic may vary, but there are some constants.

First, primary sources express original ideas and direct observation. The creators of primary sources have immediate, firsthand knowledge of the topic. If a primary source deals with the battle of Gettysburg during the American Civil War, for example, the author was actually involved (such as a soldier who fought in the battle) or observed the event directly.

Also, primary sources are contemporaneous with the topic. They are created around the same time as the events they deal with. For example, an account of the Battle of Gettysburg must have been written within a few years of the battle in order to be considered a primary source.

Because they provide firsthand accounts and descriptions of the past, primary sources are extremely useful to researchers. A well-chosen primary source can give your research paper an immediacy you can't find anywhere else. Many types of sources are considered primary. Here are some of the most common:

- **Personal accounts**, such as diaries, journals, memoirs, autobiographies, and letters; while these sources are often published long after the authors have died, they are still primary.

- **Contemporary publications**, including newspaper and magazine articles *from the period you're researching*, public letters by important people, essays, the texts of speeches, and so on; even histories and biographies can be primary sources, if they were written during the period you're researching.

- Official **records**, including legal, governmental, or business documents.

- If you're writing about art or literature, the **work itself** is a primary source. Art and literature can be useful for research papers on historical topics, too. Harriet Beecher Stowe's novel *Uncle Tom's Cabin*, for example, would be an excellent primary source for a research paper on the pre–Civil War abolition movement.

EXERCISE ONE:

IDENTIFYING PRIMARY SOURCES

Below are samples or excerpts from several potential research sources. In the space provided, indicate whether the sample is from a primary source.

1. *From:* **The unanimous Declaration of the thirteen united States of America**

— That to secure these rights, Governments are instituted among Men, deriving their just powers from the consent of the governed,—That whenever any Form of Government becomes destructive of these ends, it is the Right of the People to alter or to abolish it, and to institute new Government, laying its foundation on such principles and organizing its powers in such form, as to them shall seem most likely to effect their Safety and Happiness. Prudence, indeed, will dictate that Governments long established should not be changed for light and transient causes; and accordingly all experience hath shewn that mankind are more disposed to suffer, while evils are sufferable than to right themselves by abolishing the forms to which they are accustomed. But when a long train of abuses and usurpations, pursuing invariably the same Object evinces a design to reduce them under absolute Despotism, it is their right, it is their duty, to throw off such Government, and to provide new Guards for their future security.—Such has been the patient sufferance of these Colonies; and such is now the necessity which constrains them to alter their former Systems of Government.

Excerpted from: USHistory.org (http://www.ushistory.org/declaration/)

Is this excerpt a primary source?

Why or why not?

2. *From:* Applebaum, Estelle. Founding Fathers, State-by-State. Hyperbolic Press of Atlantis University, 1985.

> George Read, one of Delaware's three signers of the Declaration of Independence, was born on the Read family farm in Cecil County, Maryland, in 1733. At the age of fifteen, he began the study of law under John Moland of Philadelphia and was admitted to the Philadelphia Bar in 1753.

> During the course of his exemplary career, Read served on the Second Continental Congress, during which he signed the Declaration of Independence. He helped draft the Constitution of the State of Delaware, and he served as a delegate from Delaware at the Constitutional Convention in Philadelphia in 1787.

Is this excerpt a primary source?

Why or why not?

3. *From*: Sylvester, Brice. A Pictorial History of Chicago, 1770 –1900. Lansing Academic Press, 1903:

> Historians generally agree that on Sunday evening, October 8, 1871, the Chicago Fire originated in the barn of Patrick and Catherine O'Leary on the West Side of the city. Ironically, the blaze spared the O'Leary home, but much of the rest of Chicago was devastated. Before the fire died out on Tuesday, October 10, it had destroyed $192,000,000 of property in an area of approximately three and one-third square miles. Over 100,000 people were left homeless, and 300 people lost their lives.

> In November and December of 1871, the Board of Police and Fire Commissioners held an inquiry to determine the cause of the fire, as well as to debate how to improve the response of city

agencies to such a disaster in the future. The board interviewed fifty people, including Mr. and Mrs. O'Leary. Over 1,100 pages of testimony were recorded. Still, board members failed to determine the fire's cause, stating merely that they could not declare with any certainty "whether it originated from a spark blown from a chimney on that windy night, or was set on fire by human agency."

Is this excerpt a primary source?

Why or why not?

4. *From:* **A letter from William H. Carter, president of the City of Chicago Board of Public Works to his brother:**

My dear Brother,   Sunday Oct. 15, 1871

I snatch the first moment I have had since one week ago tonight. Our beautiful city is in ruins. The greatest calamity that ever befell a city is upon us.

Boastful Chicago lies prostrate and with outstretched arms in begging of her sister cities for relief. It is impossible to relate the loss of life or suffering during the conflagration or to estimate the am't of property that has been consumed....

Is this excerpt a primary source?

Why or why not?

> A **secondary source** is based on the experiences or the work of others. Secondary sources have an indirect relationship with your topic—instead of presenting the author's firsthand experiences and observations, they rely on primary sources (and other secondary sources) as their sources.

In general, secondary sources are created after the events, lives, and ideas that they address. For example, *The Autobiography of Benjamin Franklin*, because it was written by Franklin himself, is a primary source. A biography of Franklin written in 1850, a half century after his death, however, is a secondary source.

Secondary sources can't give you the immediacy of a firsthand account, but they offer broad overviews and perspectives that primary sources can't. Given the benefit of hindsight, secondary sources can interpret, evaluate, and analyze what primary sources can only report.

In a thoroughly well-researched paper, primary sources will provide the evidence in support of the thesis, and secondary sources will provide much of the commentary on that evidence. There are many different kinds of secondary sources. Here are some of the most common:

- Book-length **biographies** and **histories**, especially accounts of events or the lives of historical figures are based on primary research. They generally include research citations, such as foot or endnotes.

- **Articles** in popular magazines like *Time* and *National Geographic* and academic journals like *The Journal of African American History* are written for the general public and usually don't include lists of the sources they use. Academic articles are written for a scholarly audience, and they usually include detailed notes about their sources. Even articles in popular magazines, however, should indicate whether the material is coming from an eyewitness or participant or from someone who interviewed the eyewitness or participant.

In Exercise One earlier, the brief biography of George Read and the report on the investigation into the Great Chicago Fire were secondary sources. The information they presented was certainly valid and useful, but you would not want to base your entire paper on secondary-source research alone.

As you might guess, primary and secondary sources offer different kinds of information. You can find a wide overview of your topic in a secondary source, such as an article describing what happened at Gettysburg and explaining why it was important to the course of the Civil War. A primary source can give you a much more direct picture of what the past was really like. For example, a soldier's account of Gettysburg can put you on the ground in the middle of the battle. It's often best to start your research with secondary sources, which will get you acquainted with the "big picture" of your topic—and may also point you to primary sources.

Of course, both types of sources have their limitations as well. Primary sources, while historically closer to the topic, lack the context, historical or otherwise, of secondary sources. The authors of primary sources are not always able to provide the interpretation, evaluation, and commentary that secondary source authors can provide. Also, primary sources usually reflect the biases of their authors and the prejudices of their times.

The authors of secondary sources, on the other hand, can draw on a vast range of knowledge and have the advantage of knowing how events turned out in the end. Secondary sources are written at a distance from the people, places, and events they describe. Their authors can only draw reasonable conclusions about the past, but even the most educated guess about life a century or more ago is still a guess.

For these reasons, it's important to include both primary and secondary sources in your research. A good mix of sources will give you a richer and more balanced perspective on your topic.

EXERCISE TWO:

IDENTIFYING PRIMARY AND SECONDARY SOURCES

Read the following excerpts from potential sources. In the space provided, explain what type of source (encyclopedia, journal, magazine article, etc.) each excerpt is most likely from. Identify whether the source is **primary** or **secondary** and explain why. Then, explain what the benefits and disadvantages of using each source might be.

1. The Confederate States of America had lost not only their military advantage, but their political standing as well. While the battle was nearing its end in Pennsylvania, Confederate Vice President Alexander Stephens was approaching the Union lines in Norfolk, Virginia, under a flag of truce. Stephens had been authorized by Confederate President Jefferson Davis to negotiate only an exchange of prisoners, but historian James M. McPherson suggests that Stephens had begun to formulate his own plan to effect peace between the North and South. Davis's original hope was that Stephens would march on Washington from the south while General Lee's army, victorious in Pennsylvania, approached from the north. The Confederacy's decisive defeat at Gettysburg, however, not only altered the way in which President Lincoln would deal with the rebellious South, it also ended any hope of the South's being recognized as a legitimate independent nation by any European capital.

    Reprinted from the fictional web site: http://en.wilkinspeedio.org/ Battle_of_Gettysburg

Is this excerpt most likely from a primary or a secondary source?

How do you know?

What might be some of the advantages of using this source?

What might be some of the disadvantages of using this source?

2.

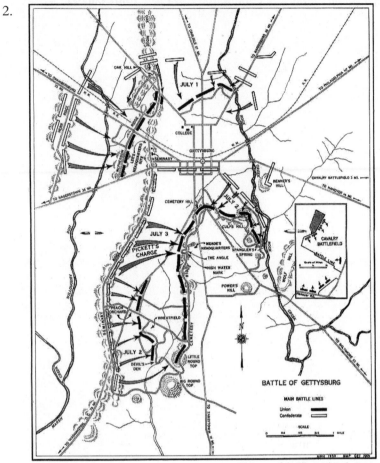

Courtesy of the National Park Service

Is this image most likely from a primary or a secondary source?

How do you know?

What might be some of the advantages of using this source?

What might be some of the disadvantages of using this source?

3. The soyle is most plentifull, sweete, whole some, and fruitfull
   of all other, there are about 14. severall sorts of sweete swelling
   tymber trees: the most parts of the underwood, Bayes and
   such like: such Okes as we, but far greater and better. After this
   acquaintance, my selfe with seaven more went twenty myle into
   the River Occam, that runneth toward the Cittie Skicoack, and
   the evening following we came to an Ile called Roanoak, from
   the harbour where we entred 7. leagues; at the North end was 9.
   houses, builded with Cedar, fortified round with sharpe trees, and
   the entrance like a Turnpik. When we came towards it, the wife
   of Granganameo came running out to meete us, (her husband
   was absent) commanding her people to draw our Boat ashore for
   beating in the billowes...

   From: "The Generall Historie of Virginia, New England & the Summer Isles" by
   Captain John Smith.

Is this excerpt most likely from a primary or a secondary source?

How do you know?

What might be some of the advantages of using this source?

What might be some of the disadvantages of using this source?

Ella's Search for Sources:

Ella knows she needs to find both primary and secondary sources. *The assignment does not specify the need for primary source material, but Ella knows that she will have, at best, a mediocre paper if she uses only secondary sources.*

She is, however, concerned about finding primary sources on the Jamestown settlement in Virginia. How much did the actual settlers in Jamestown and the Native Americans they met write down? How much of that historical record survives? Where might she be able to access this information? What *other* primary sources might she be able to utilize?

The first thing Ella does is sit down at her computer to search the Internet. We'll talk more about the benefits and disadvantages of Internet research; right now, we'll simply examine how Ella begins her search for material for her paper.

Because this is an *academic research paper*, Ella knows she must broaden her search for sources to include more than just the most popular search engines. By using Subject Directories like the ones listed below, she can tap into **relevant and credible** sources.

> **Search Engines**
>
> - Google (www.Google.com)
> - Yahoo! Search (search.yahoo.com)
> - Ask.com (www.ask.com)
> - Live Search (live.com)
> - MSN (www.msn.com)

> **Subject Directories**
>
> - Librarians' Internet Index (www.lii.org)
> - Internet Public Library (www.ipl.org)
> - Open directory (www.dmoz.org)

> **Meta-Search Engines**
>
> - Clusty (www.clusty.com)
> - Dogpile (www.dogpile.com)
> - Excite! (www.excite.com)
> - MetaCrawler (www.metacrawler.com)
> - SurfWax (www.surfwax.com)
>
> - WebCrawler (www.webcrawler.com)

Don't worry if you don't know the difference between these types of engines. We'll be discussing them in greater detail on pages 88-97.

For her search, Ella is likely to begin with search terms like:

Jamestown

Jamestown, Virginia

Jamestown Colony

Virginia Company

London Company

Plymouth Company

Powhatan

As she continues, however, some of her early results will suggest other words and phrases she might want to search for.

Among the potential sources she finds in her first search:

The Virtual Jamestown Archive is, "...a digital research, teaching and learning project that explores the legacies of the Jamestown settlement and 'the Virginia experiment.'" Includes maps, labor contracts, public records, **firsthand accounts and letters**, and a reference center featuring a timeline and biographies (including Pocahontas, Captain John Smith, and Chief Powhatan). **A collaboration between Virginia Tech, the University of Virginia, and the Virginia Center for Digital History.** URL: http://www.virtualjamestown.org/

Clearly, the promise of "firsthand accounts and letters" suggests that Ella will find some useful primary source material here. The fact that the site is a collaboration between two highly respected Virginia schools suggests that the information will be reliable and credible, as well.

Colonists and Native Americans "offers historical documents: *'Texts and Archives: ... History of Jamestowne (Jamestowne Society)/ ... The Real Pocahontas by Jessica Ronky* (Times) ... This Web site is a part of the *Texts and Documents project at Hanover College.* URL: http://history.hanover.edu/project. html#17

Again, the promise of "historical documents" and archival information suggests that Ella will find some primary source material here, as well. As is the case with the above source, this site is maintained by a respectable college and is, therefore, credible and reliable.

As Ella continues her Internet search, she should scan the sites whose descriptions sound promising. Then, she should either bookmark the site or, even better, begin to compile an organized listing of potentially useful sites to examine later.

POTENTIAL PRIMARY SOURCES:

1. http://www.virtualjamestown.org/— *maps, labor contracts, public records, firsthand accounts and letters, and a reference center featuring a timeline and biographies—Virginia Tech, UVA, and Virginia Center for Digital History*

2. http://history.hanover.edu/project.html#17/

   Archival information
   Jamestowne Society
   Ronky, Jessica. The Real Pocahontas
   —Hanover College

3. http://home.wi.rr.com/rickgardiner/primarysources.htm — *"The American Colonist's Library: A Treasury of Primary Source Documents: A massive collection of the literature and documents which were most relevant to the colonists' lives in America"*

7. http://www.kidinfo.com/American_History/Colonization_Jamestown.html — *seems kind of juvenile, but has some potentially useful links, e.g., "The American Colonist's Library."*

8. http://www.historyisfun.org/Jamestown-Settlement.htm — *"Jamestown Settlement, living-history museum of early America." — seems to be sort of an online, virtual museum, very touristy, fairly basic (tertiary) information, geared mostly for children.*

Chances are, of course, that Ella will not be able to limit herself to only Internet research, but remember that the key to a top-notch research paper is *the quality of the information* not the delivery system. John Smith's diary is John Smith's diary, whether you are reading an electronic version online or poring over a fifty-year-old photograph of the page with a magnifying glass.

Still, there is a great deal of archival material that has not yet been digitalized. Many scholarly journals do not publish their articles online, and many interesting and valuable books are no longer in print and exist only in libraries.

Ella should not forget the potentially valuable information she might be able to gain from conducting interviews with experts on her topic, or what she might learn by an actual visit to Jamestown.

The key is to make certain that she looks for and finds all of the information she needs from *credible sources.*

EXERCISE THREE:

COMPILING YOUR OWN LIST OF POTENTIAL SOURCES

Now, apply what you have learned and practiced to your own research assignment. Using any or all of the Search Engines, Subject Directories, and Meta-Search Engines, begin to compile a list of potential sources with comments, as Ella did above.

1. List some of the search words and phrases you will use:

2. Follow the format below and record the potential sources you find and take notes on their probable usefulness.

URL:

Site Title:

Site Contents:

NOTES:

Site Maintained By / Source(s):

10. What are "relevant" and "credible" sources?

No matter what your topic is, you'll have plenty of information to work with. But not all information is equal. When you're sick, you don't go to the auto mechanic, and when your car breaks down, you don't take it to the doctor. Likewise, if the problem with your car is with the brakes, you don't necessarily need to know your windshield washer fluid is low. Nor do you need the doctor to X-ray your foot when you've gone in for a migraine headache.

The issues in all of the above cases amount to (1) whether or not the source is able to provide you with information that will be useful to you **(relevant),** and (2) whether or not that source is even in a position to provide information on that particular topic **(credible).**

Early on, we defined a research paper as "a thesis-driven essay that uses **relevant, credible sources** to support its ideas and arguments."

> A source is **relevant** if it has information about your topic. Sources that increase your understanding and help you develop your thesis are valuable and worth your effort. A source that gives you an overview of your topic with few details to enrich your thesis is less relevant, but still useful. A source that has little or nothing to do with your topic is *irrelevant.* It won't help you develop your thesis, and it's a waste of your time.

A source that seems to contradict your preliminary thesis is also relevant. Remember that you allowed for the possibility that your research would prove your initial ideas to be incorrect. Thus, any **credible** source that makes you rethink your thesis is highly valuable.

How do you determine a source's relevance? First, when you glance at a website's summary on your search engine, or glance briefly at the site itself, you can develop a sense of whether or not that source's information is going to be useful. Second, when you glance at a book's description, reviews on shopping sites like Amazon.com, a review in a magazine or newspaper, or even the blurb on the book's back cover, you can gain a sense of the book's relevance. Finally, a quick scan of a table of contents, index, or some of the source's material will give you an idea of the information that book is offering.

Ultimately, however, the test of whether or not the information is relevant is the extent to which it helps you clarify and support your thesis. No matter how interesting it might be to examine George Washington's private life, his relationships with his wife and step-children, an intimately personal biography will not help you argue the importance of Washington's role as Commander-in-Chief of the Continental Army.

> **Credibility** is essentially whatever allows you to believe (and to assure your reader) that your source is in a position to know what he or she is talking about. Most doctors display their degrees and certifications to establish their credibility with their patients. Mechanics also display their credentials to assure their customers that they know what they're doing when it comes to repairing cars.

Someone with a degree in United States History (and the higher the degree, the better) is a much more credible source for information on the Jamestown Colony than the entertainer hired as the spokesperson for a series of "Visit Jamestown" television commercials. The archivist who has devoted years to studying original documents—letters, diaries, etc.—and commenting on them is a more credible source than the high school student who has read the commentaries and written a report on them.

The questions to ask yourself when evaluating any potential source for its credibility are: "How probable is it that the creator of this source knows what he or she is talking about? Why should I trust that information from this source is accurate and current?"

How do you determine a source's credibility? There are several indicators of credibility that you must consider when preparing to write a research paper. The higher the stakes connected with your research paper—your grade for the marking period, your grade for the course, your degree or certification—the more it is in your best interest to be able to state with confidence that your sources are all credible.

1. **Look at the author.** Who is he or she? What is the author's profession? What degrees, certificates, education, or experience does the author have? *What puts the author in a position to speak authoritatively on this subject?*

   If the source you're evaluating is a book, you can usually find information about the author at the beginning or end. Journals often include some information about the authors of articles; magazines occasionally do also.

   If you're at a loss, do a quick Internet search on the author.

   If the source does not list an author, or if you can find *no* information on the author, then you absolutely must question the source's credibility.

2. **Look at the source itself.** Who is behind the production or publication of the information? A magazine like *National Geographic* is produced by a well-respected foundation that has funded scientific research and global exploration for over a century. Popular gossip tabloids are not backed by such reputable agencies.

   Academic journals are rarely well known, but are usually linked to reputable institutions—colleges and universities, research institutes, and the like. For example, the journal *Early American History* is published by the McNeil Center for Early American Studies at the University of Pennsylvania. Several of the Internet sources Ella found in her search were produced by respected colleges and universities in Virginia and Indiana.

   Credibility is a special concern online because many websites are completely unreliable. Should you rule out online articles altogether? Of course not—but, just as you know you would rule out a print tabloid as a potential source in favor of an academic journal, you should exclude popular web sites that are not linked to respected and reputable agencies or institutions.

Primary sources are, by their very nature, highly credible, and you do not need to worry about the credentials of the author. A general's account of a battle is no more credible than a foot soldier's—both witnessed the same event, even if their perspectives are different. *In fact, being able to present two different, but equally credible points of view can only make your paper stronger.* The credibility of a primary source lies in its authenticity. If historical periodicals and documents are authentic, they're credible. The best way to certify a source's authenticity is to know who is providing the source to you: a respected institution? an obscure agency? a completely unidentified agency?

If you cannot find a clear statement of the source's affiliation (whether a print source or an electronic site), then, you absolutely must question that source's credibility.

How does Ella evaluate her potential sources?

We saw in the previous section that Ella had already begun evaluating her potential sources. She considered the type of information the source was likely to yield, the intended audience for the source (and, therefore, its usefulness to her), and so on.

Now, let's look at the notes she has taken while considering the relevance and credibility of each of her potential sources.

Source 1:

Type of source: *Web Site*

Title: *The Virtual Jamestown Archive*

URL (or other identification as applicable): *http://www. virtualjamestown.org/*

Description: *"...a digital research, teaching and learning project that explores the legacies of the Jamestown settlement and 'the Virginia experiment.' Includes maps, labor contracts, public records, firsthand accounts and letters, and a reference center featuring a timeline and biographies (including Pocahontas, Captain John Smith, and Chief Powhatan). A collaboration between Virginia Tech, the University of Virginia, and the Virginia Center for Digital History."*

Is this source relevant? *Yes*

Why or why not? *The "legacy" of the "Virginia Experiment" will certainly include the impact of the failures and successes of this plantation/colony on the development of future colonies. The "legacy" will also include Jamestown's influence on the development of the United States.*

Is this source credible? *Yes*

Why or why not? *The site is maintained by three highly respected and prestigious schools and foundations. The source also contains primary source material: firsthand accounts, letters, etc.*

Source 2:

Type of source: *Website*

Title: *Colonists and Native Americans*

URL (or other identification as applicable): *http://history.hanover.edu/ project.html#17*

Description: *Archives contain the full texts of: History of Jamestowne (Jamestowne Society), The Real Pocahontas by Jessica Ronky (Times)*

This Website is a part of the Texts and Documents project at Hanover College."

Is this source relevant? *Probably*

Why or why not? *Among the changes that had to be made for the survival of Jamestown—that had an impact on the formation of future colonies—were the ways the settlers interacted with the Native Americans whose lands the settlers occupied.*

To learn something about the historical Pocahontas might provide insight into European-Native American relations.

Is this source credible? *Yes*

Why or why not? *The site is maintained by a respected academic institution.*

As Ella continues her search for sources, therefore, she assesses each one for its potential usefulness. She still keeps her record of sources she does not expect to be useful, but Ella is developing a sense of what sources she will examine first, and which she will not bother with unless she has a need and sufficient time before her due date.

EXERCISE FOUR:

PRACTICING EVALUATING POTENTIAL SOURCES

You've been helping Rob with his research assignment. Now, help him identify which of his potential sources are likely to be relevant and credible, and which are not likely to be helpful to him.

NOTE: Sources identified with an asterisk * have been created and should not be taken as genuine.

Rob

Focused Topic: How the development of the railroads increased the movement west and changed the nature of those who went.

Preliminary Thesis: Without the construction of the Transcontinental Railroad in 1869, the United States of America could quite possibly have developed east-west differences even more significant than those that divided the northern and southern states.

Potential Source 1:

National Public Radio Broadcast: Experiencing America

http://www.npr.org/klbj/exam/rbeature/rb_interview.html

In this interview, Don Simpkins, Distinguished Professor of Native American History at Oklahoma State University, discusses the American West before white European settlement and the impact of the railroad on Native American life, focusing especially on the near-extinction of the American buffalo.

Is this source relevant?

Why or why not?

Is this source credible?

Why or why not?

Potential Source 2:

First North American Transcontinental Railroad Photographic Virtual Museum:

"A Tribute to the Contributions of Chinese-Americans to the First North American Transcontinental Railroad"*

http://cprr.org/Museum/Chinese.html

Description: Photographs, texts of speeches and tributes, and assorted quotations. Bibliography of references and links to other sites.

Is this source relevant?

Why or why not?

Is this source credible?

Why or why not?

Potential Source 3:

> Book: Poole, Victor H. *The Tenuous Relationship between the Government of the United States of America and the Railroads of the Pacific States. New York: Greene and Greyhound, 1871.* *

> From the blurb about the book on Congobooks.com: "It is impossible to discuss, with depth and insight, the matter of the relationship between the government of the United States of America and the various railroad companies of the various Pacific states, with respect to their legal rights and obligations, under and by virtue of the various Acts allowing for the incorporation of said railroad companies, without full and careful consideration paid to the condition of the Country at the time of the passage of said law..."

Is this source relevant?

Why or why not?

Is this source credible?

Why or why not?

Potential Source 4:

Book: Prescott, Ansun. ed. *There Went the Neighborhood: The Collected Diaries of Marjorie Holmestead 1850 - 1900.* San Francisco: Books by the Bay, Inc., 2005. *

From the blurb about the book on Congobooks.com: "Lovingly edited by the diarist's great-grandson, who still lives in the house built by Marjorie and her husband, this book is the vivid first-person account of a young girl's journey west to build a new life and the challenges she faced in an ever-changing world."

Is this source relevant?

Why or why not?

Is this source credible?

Why or why not?

EXERCISE FIVE:

EVALUATING YOUR OWN POTENTIAL SOURCES

Now, apply to your own research assignment what you have learned and practiced.

Look at the sources you collected in Exercise Three (as well as any additional sources you may have collected since then) and use the spaces that follow to consider each source's relevance and credibility.

Focused Topic:

Preliminary Thesis:

Potential Source 1:

Type of source:

Title:

URL (or other identification as applicable):

Description:

Is this source relevant?

Why or why not?

Is this source credible?

Why or why not?

One last issue that needs to be addressed as we talk about the relevance and credibility of potential sources is **bias. To what extent does bias render a source unusable?**

First of all, let's examine what bias is and how possible it is to find a completely unbiased source. Typically, bias is defined as any tendency, inclination, or preference for one particular outlook, ideology, or result. In its purest form, bias is inescapable. The information you will be dealing with in your research project, regardless of the delivery medium, comes from a human being who will inevitably be affected by his or her particular tendencies, inclinations, and preferences. Each of us has a unique viewpoint largely shaped by our gender, age, race, geography, and so on. Any truth we see, we see from our own viewpoint, and any truth we explain, we can explain only in terms we understand. There is, therefore, a degree of bias in every bit of information you will examine. There will be bias in your final research paper. To some extent, your preliminary thesis already reflects that bias.

In its least pure form, bias is synonymous with prejudice and will severely weaken—if not completely destroy—your argument if you do not recognize it and deal with it appropriately.

Consider two primary sources' accounts of the same battle. One is written by the general who led the successful charge. The second is written by a private on the losing side who lost his leg in the retreat. Can you imagine how, even if each sets out to tell a "truthful" account of the battle, each account will be radically different?

The key to good research is not to eliminate both sources due to bias and keep searching for an "unbiased account." You'll never find one. The key is to be aware of the bias in both accounts and present them both in an attempt to present a "complete" account of the battle.

Even a strong, blatant bias is not necessarily a bad thing.

Look at one of the United States' hottest and longest-running debates: gun control. Members of the National Rifle Association are clearly biased in favor of *not* regulating a private citizen's right to purchase and own a gun. They interpret the Second Amendment to the Constitution to mean that there will never be such a law. On the other hand, gun-control advocates interpret the same amendment to mean that no law will ever prevent a state from maintaining its own militia, and that an individual's right to own a gun *can* (and should) be regulated.

On both sides of the debate, opinions are strong, and emotions run high. Both sides can present factual information, statistics, eye-witness accounts, and expert testimony to support their view. There will be no problem with using information from either side in your paper as long as (1) you recognize that the information you are presenting is biased and (2) the source itself does not *intentionally misrepresent those facts, statistics, etc., in an attempt to bolster its argument.*

Bias becomes a problem only when the source lies, misrepresents facts, ignores vital information, misinterprets data, or doesn't even provide the data that are the basis of its interpretations.

Look at some of the sources Ella has been using and decide how biased each is and the extent to which that bias might render the source unusable.

How does one evaluate bias and its impact on the usability of a

---

From Ella's Notes

Goddard, Woodward, Ph. D. <u>Economics of Early North American Settlements.</u> Princeton, NJ: Princeton University Press, 2005.

FROM INTRO, P. IV: "This book provides an in-depth study of the often tense, always shifting relationship between the Crown, the investors, and the settlers in Britain's first attempts at North American Colonists. What began in 1606 as a purely profit-minded, commercial exploit became, by 1620, a self-sufficient community claiming equality with any village or hamlet in England herself."

FROM INTRO: P. XIX: "James [I, king of England at the time— the colony of Jamestown was named for him] prohibited the colonists' selling their tobacco directly to other countries. All foreign sales were made through London—and were heavily taxed, severely lessening the colonists' profit on their crop. This was the first colonial dissatisfaction that would eventually contribute to the American Revolution."

FROM CHAPTER 3, P. 173: *"Despite the years of effort and expanded investment on the part of those who sought to grow rich on the Virginia Experiment, Jamestown had not yet found a crop, mineral, or industry that would make it economically viable. The Virginia Company continued to pour people and resources into a venture with no return on its investment, nor any real hope of one in the foreseeable future.*

Finally, in 1612 John Rolfe decided to grow tobacco. The strain of tobacco grown by the Natives, Nicotiana Rustica, was too harsh for British tastes, so Rolfe instead grew the milder Nicotiana Tabacum, the strain being grown for Spain in Trinidad and South America."

Ella decides to keep *Economics of Early North American Settlements*. The information presented, while a bit general, is presented in an objective, non-biased tone, and comes from a credible source.

FROM CHAPTER 3, P. 175: *"As it was a capital offense in Spain and her colonies to give or sell the coveted Nicotiana Tabacum seeds to a non-Spaniard, it is not known how Rolfe managed to procure them. Still, it was providential for his beloved colony that he did."*

FROM CHAPTER 35, P. 241: *"James I had despised tobacco and its use and disapproved of the colony's dependence on this single crop for its economic survival. However, he was vain enough also to realize that, if the colony that bore his name were to survive, the tobacco trade would have to continue—even increase. Likewise, the king was greedy enough to realize the tremendous amount of money Virginia's growing tobacco trade was pouring into his treasury."*

The United States and Moral Compromise. 23 March 2001. No affiliated organization or institution cited. 1 April, 2008 <http://www.morallycompromised.com.

"The seeds of America's damnation were first sown in 1612 when John Rolfe planted the cursed tobacco, intending it to be the "salvation" of his struggling Jamestown. Knowing that the weaker, less-exhilarating _Nicotiana Rustica_ that the local Indians grew would never sell in London, Rolfe stole seeds for the highly potent _Nicotiana Tabacum_. This was the strain being grown in Trinidad and South America, and, as it was a capital offense in Spain and her colonies to give or sell these coveted seeds to any non-Spaniard, Rolfe could not have acquired them by any legitimate means."

With its lack of affiliation, absence of a stated author, potentially inflammatory language like "damnation," and "profane and pagan," and its misrepresentation of facts (e.g., how Rolfe acquired the seeds he used, the suggestion that the Natives' strain of tobacco was 'weaker,' etc.), Ella decides this source is too biased and unreliable.

"...Pocahontas knew a good deal about the cultivation and curing of tobacco—and knew where to learn what she did not know. Thus, the conclusion that tobacco was a profane and pagan plant with which the savage population of the Americas seduced their European liberators is not as far-fetched as some history-revisionists would suggest."

"By 1619 Jamestown had exported over ten tons of tobacco. So wealthy had the avaricious colonists become that they were able to afford an import that would assure the country's doom: African blacks, who, though they were not yet chattel slaves, would soon enough devolve into this lowest of social classes."

<u>Seekers of Truth in History</u>. 01 April 1984. Americans for Truth, Justice, and the American Way. 05 May 2008 <http://www. truthhistory.org.*

"Perhaps the hardest lesson we learn by examining both sides is that the heroes of history were, in their own day, mere human beings living the best they knew how, playing the hands they'd been dealt the best they could. James I abhorred the exportation of Virginian tobacco, but it kept his colony alive and made him rich. George Washington hated owning slaves, but he was loath to free the ones he could and separate families in the process..."

Ella is uncertain about this website, as she can find no information about the Americans for Truth, Justice, and the American Way. The information they present, however, is valid and seems fairly objective in tone and presentation, so she does not exclude it altogether.

"One should, perhaps, forgive John Rolfe for his adamant advocacy of tobacco. Certainly, in 1612, no one knew of addiction and health risks associated with tobacco smoke or the habit of 'dipping' snuff. In fact, based on the evidence they had from the Powhatans, smoking tobacco was actually a healthful and spiritual activity."

"The fact of the matter is that none of the good the United States has brought to the world would have been possible without the bad. The West's addiction to tobacco has certainly been an ongoing social ill, but, had the Jamestown Colony been allowed to fail, there may have been no United States to begin with. The introduction of slave labor into the nation that would come to typify freedom is a blot that will never be totally expunged, yet the fight to end freedom and the fights for equality that have continued to the present day have served only to strengthen the nation's ideals and serve as inspirations to oppressed people around the world..."

source?

Determining bias in a source is a relatively easy process, especially if you remember that virtually every source is biased to some degree. The question becomes, then, not whether the source is biased, but in what direction and to what extent.

When evaluating a source for bias, answer the following questions and use your answers to determine whether the source is still usable:

1. **What is the stated purpose of the source?**

   Consider whether the book or magazine's primary purpose is to educate, inform, or entertain.

   Is the newspaper article you are considering a news item? Feature article? Editorial? Letter to the editor?

   Is a television or film documentary primarily informative or entertaining?

   The ever-popular television "infomercial" is a purely commercial medium. The producers have a product or service to sell.

   Some sites, especially those maintained by colleges, universities, or other purely academic institutions (.edu), do exist simply to provide information. Others, while maintaining the overall appearance of an informational site, are more commercial in nature. Still others are blatantly persuasive in nature, providing their information with the sole purpose (expressed or not) of forwarding their agenda.

2. **Who are the producers of the source, and what are their intentions?**

   Examine the author(s) of the book(s) you are considering. Who are they, and what are their affiliations? What agenda might they have? Why would they have chosen to write the book?

   Who are the publishers or producers? Many organizations publish periodicals and newsletters for their memberships. Take into consideration potential bias in informational articles appearing in the magazines produced by the National Rifle Association, the American Association of Retired Persons, the National Wildlife Federation, Greenpeace, etc. Are you likely to get a full and objective view from any of these publications?

3. Who is the intended audience of the source?

You must be able to recognize that a book, magazine, film, television program, website, or any other information source geared toward a particular demographic is probably going to be biased toward that demographic. Your opinions on any subject a biased source may present are not relevant; you may agree with the source or disagree with it, but it's the *source* you need to evaluate, not your personal feelings or beliefs.

4. How factual and specific is the information provided in the source?

The difference between facts and other bits of information is that facts are not open to interpretation. The sky is blue. Green plants take in carbon dioxide (CO_2) and give off oxygen (O_2). The geographic North Pole and the magnetic North Pole are not the same. Facts are *verifiable*, which means you should be able to find the same (or very similar) facts in a variety of different sources. *If one source's "facts" are radically different from the other sources you've consulted, suspect bias.*

The more specific a source is, the more difficult it is to mask bias. To say that two-thirds of all of the original Jamestown settlers died the first year due to tobacco-related illness is either true or not. If it is found to be *untrue*, then the source becomes suspect. To say, however, that "most" of the settlers died is a little more difficult to prove or disprove, depending on the actual numbers. To say "many died" is even more difficult to prove or disprove, since "many" is a vague word subject to interpretation. The more your potential source relies on vague terms that are subject to interpretation (like "many"), the more you should suspect bias.

Some words and phrases are completely subjective and open to interpretation. To say that "too many" settlers died... is a conclusion, an opinion, not a fact. (How many is "too many"? One? Twelve? More than fifty percent?)

Your sources certainly have the right to interpret the facts they present, and they will almost always express opinions on their topics. The key to determining whether the sources' bias disqualifies them from being used in your paper is whether they *show the specific, factual information* on which their conclusion is based or simply assert their conclusion.

5. How balanced is the specific, factual information presented by the source?

You've heard the adage that there are at least two sides to every story. You already realize that two or three eyewitnesses to the same event will relate considerably different versions of the event. Therefore, a thoroughly reliable and unbiased source will make it a point to share the accounts of more than one eyewitness.

There are facts and statistics about private citizens' use of handguns to defend themselves and their families, which could be used to support the NRA's position that gun control laws are not necessary. There are likewise facts and statistics about private citizens being assaulted in their own homes and killed by their own weapons, which could be used to support gun control advocates' contentions that private citizens should not be allowed to own handguns.

A truly unbiased source will present both. If the *only* factual information you are given supports only one side of the issue, the source is biased.

6. Does the source list its sources?

Just as you will have to disclose to your reader where you got the information you are using in support of your thesis, your sources should disclose that information to you. If they do not (or if their sources seem suspect), be wary of bias.

NOTE: It is, however, perfectly allowable for your source to interpret the contradictory data in a way that supports his or her thesis—this is using a rhetorical device called PROCATALEPSIS. You're allowed to use the same technique in your paper. The point is, however, that an unbiased source will mention facts from both sides of the issue.

All in all, however, the issue is not whether a given source is biased—nearly every source you encounter will be—but how you deal with that bias in supporting your own thesis:

> **Do not use material from blatantly biased sources.**

Whether the source is print or electronic, if you know it was produced by an individual or group with an agenda, do not use it. Many legitimate and, therefore, unbiased sources will provide you with useful information; it is simply not worth risking a lower grade by including biased material.

> **Present a balance of information from a variety of sources.**

The data you got from the *NRA Today* article is absolutely verifiable fact. Good. Now, make sure you have some verifiably factual information from the *Guns No More Monthly*. Remember that the rhetorical device called PROCATALEPSIS allows you to state evidence that contradicts your thesis and discuss it in order to show its flaws, thus strengthening your own argument.

> **Verify *every* fact from *every* source with at least one or two other sources.**

Good journalists do this. Good researchers do, too. It's one reason research papers are usually so long and contain listings of so many sources. If you base your entire argument on a single fact from a single source, and that fact is shown to be untrue and the source thoroughly biased, what are you left with? What kind of grade would your paper deserve?

> **Acknowledge the bias that you know is present in the source.**

You know that the television talk show whose transcript you're quoting is produced *by* women, *for* women, with an exclusively female panel and *only* female guests. Be honest with yourself and your reader and acknowledge the probability of bias up front. Then, explain why the information is still valid and helpful to your thesis.

EXERCISE SIX:

LOOKING FOR BIAS IN POTENTIAL SOURCES

You've been helping Rob with his research assignment. Now, help him determine whether his potential sources are biased and whether they might still be useful.

Rob

Focused Topic: How the development of the railroads increased the movement west and changed the nature of those who went.

Preliminary Thesis: Without the construction of the Transcontinental Railroad in 1869, the United States of America could quite possibly have developed east-west differences even more significant than those that divided the northern and southern states.

Potential Source 1:

The *History of United States Imperialism: 1803 - 1898.* 01 February 2002. The Buckworthy Institute. 11 May 2008 <http://www. buckworthyinstitute.org>.*

> The Indian Removal Act of 1830 authorized President Andrew Jackson to negotiate treaties that would exchange tribal land in the East for western lands that had been acquired in the Louisiana Purchase.

> President Jackson actively promoted this policy, citing national security as his primary concern.

> Great Britain and Spain had, in the recent past, allied themselves with—and armed—Native Americans living within U.S. borders in order to wage war with the United States.

> Numerous Indian Removal treaties were signed, and the majority of American Indians reluctantly but peacefully complied.

> China's defeat in the First Opium War (1840—1842) contributed to a fairly large wave of Chinese immigrants fleeing the deteriorating cultural and economic conditions in their country.

> The Mexican-American War (1846-1848) was motivated in large part by southern Democrats' belief in the Manifest Destiny of the United States.

> The Mexican Empire included what is now California, Nevada, Utah, northern Arizona, western Colorado, southwestern Wyoming, New Mexico, and Texas.

> Even today, these southwestern states maintain a strong Spanish influence in their language, food, and architecture.

> 300,000 white settlers crossed the country, headed for California in the 1848—1855 Gold Rush.

> The 1849 Gold Rush also created a second wave of Chinese immigrants seeking their fortunes.

> California entered the United States as the thirty-first state in 1850.

> The population of California in 1850 was approximately 40% Spanish, 40% Native American, 10% Chinese, and 10% white American.

Is this source biased?

Why or why not?

Can this source be used?

Why or why not?

Potential Source 2:

Website: *Divergent Views of American History.* 10 October 1998. Department of Alternative Studies, University of Saint Michaels. 15 May 2008 <http://www.stmichaelsme.edu/altstu/amhist>.*

> The Central Pacific Railroad's business ethic was such that whatever would help to complete the western portion of the railroad on time and on budget would be implemented.

For this reason, work crews were segregated to allow Chinese laborers to work together and communicate in their own language.

CPRR managers also noticed the Chinese management style (allowing the men who were *actually doing the work* to determine how best to do it) and adopted it for all of their work crews. Production from all of the work crews increased with this decreased interference from the management.

> The work was strenuous and the conditions harsh. Many workers perished during the harsh winters and blistering summers.

> Due to the difficulty of their work, Chinese and Irish laborers were paid the generous sum of nearly a dollar a day.

> Because the diet to which they were accustomed was so different from the European-American workers', the Chinese were not forced to eat the food provided by the camps. Instead, they were allowed to cook their own meals, often consisting of fish, dried oysters, fruit, mushrooms, and seaweed.

> A team of both Chinese and Irish laborers—chosen for their proven speed and thoroughness—was selected to lay the final ten miles of track. This momentous task was accomplished in the record time of only twelve hours.

Is this source biased?

Why or why not?

Can this source be used?

Why or why not?

Potential Source 3:

Book: Cho, Raymond. *The Noble Chinese and the American Nation.* San Francisco: Allworld Press, 1985.*

> Chinese laborers struggled for the paltry sum of $28 per month

> Their very dangerous work included blasting with nitroglycerine they had to make themselves on site and laying ties over the treacherous terrain of the high Sierras.

> 1,330 Chinese martyrs lost their lives while building the western route of the railroad.

> At mealtimes they were segregated from the other workers and subsisted on a meager diet of seaweed and fungus.

> To tunnel through the mountains and lay track up steep inclines, the Chinese employed engineering methods known only to them, all of which remained a mystery to the whites for whom they were working.

> Because of their superior work ethic, a Chinese crew was chosen to lay the final ten miles of track, and they completed the task in a previously unheard of twelve hours.

Is this source biased?

Why or why not?

Can this source be used?

Why or why not?

Potential Source 4:

Book: Prescott, Ansun. ed. *There Went the Neighborhood: The Collected Diaries of Marjorie Holmestead 1850 - 1900.* San Francisco: Books by the Bay, Inc., 2005.*

"Thank goodness for the new railroad! Now I finally have normal neighbors and civilized people with whom I can have a civil conversation. Those brute Indian women may have been generous with their food and medicine and homespun cloth, but I do not trust the look in their beady, little eyes when they study the nice things Charles and I brought out west with us. They'll kill us in our sleep for my china and crystal as sure as anything. And those Chinamen! Saints preserve us, if I have to listen to another word of their nasal jibberish! I do wish the trains weren't so full of filthy, drunken men wanting nothing more than to get rich with a gold strike, but the girls that have come are right nice and clean and neighborly. California might still become a proper state one day!"

Is this source biased?

Why or why not?

Can this source be used?

Why or why not?

EXERCISE SEVEN:

EVALUATING YOUR OWN POTENTIAL SOURCES FOR BIAS

Now, apply to your own research assignment what you have learned and practiced.

Look at some of the sources you collected in Exercise Three. Then, use the spaces below to discuss each source's bias and usability.

Source:

Write down the information for this source as modeled in Ella's and Rob's papers.

Jot down some notes, especially quotations that you feel are representative of the information presented in the source, the source's tone, etc.

Is this source biased?

Why or why not?

Can this source be used?

Why or why not?

11. Where can I find the sources I need?

Now that you know what you're looking for in sources, it's time for you to start your research in earnest. However, where should you look? Where are all these sources we've been talking about? You're likely to find most of the sources you need in two places: the library and the Internet.

> As we've already mentioned, the **Internet** is a powerful research tool. But to use it effectively, you must be selective and critical.

Online, you can find articles; databases; encyclopedias, dictionaries, and other reference materials; the archives of magazines and newspapers; research data; excerpts from and full texts of old books that are not copyright protected and may be unavailable in print; government documents; and much, much more. You can look up definitions or verify historical dates, but there's so much information—and so much of it is unreliable—that it's easy to get overwhelmed.

When conducting your online search, you'll want to explore all three information retrieval systems the Web makes available to you.

A **search engine** is an information retrieval system—not unlike an electronic research assistant—designed to help find information stored on computer systems like the World Wide Web. Search engines greatly reduce the time needed to find information. This information may consist of websites, images, and other types of files. Many also search for information in newsgroups, databases, or open directories.

The most common and popular search engines are:

- Google (www.Google.com)
- Yahoo! Search (www.search.yahoo.com)
- Ask.com (www.ask.com)
- Live Search (www.live.com)
- MSN (www.msn.com)

Meta-Search Engines operate on the notion that the Web is too large for any one engine to search it all and provide you with fully comprehensive search results. Therefore, a meta-search engine sends your request to several other search engines and/or databases and collects the results into a single list. The benefit of using a meta-search engine is that you enter your search term only once and gather potential sources from several search engines at the same time. This saves you the time and effort of having to use multiple search engines separately.

The most popular meta-search engines include:

- Clusty (clusty.com)
- Dogpile (www.dogpile.com)
- Excite! (www.excite.com)
- MetaCrawler (www.metacrawler.com)
- SurfWax (www.surfwax.com)
- WebCrawler (www.webcrawler.com)

A subject directory differs from a search engine in that search engines are programmed to conduct their searches electronically, while subject directories are collected and organized by humans. The benefit to searching on a subject directory is that you are more likely to find academic sources that might not appear on the search engine (or might come up as the three-millionth source in a list of three million!). You are also likely to find more useful referrals to other sources of information than on the sites a search engine will find for you.

The main disadvantage is that your search will probably produce fewer "hits."

The most common and usable subject directories are:

- Librarians' Internet Index (www.lii.org)
- Internet Public Library (www.ipl.org)
- Open directory (www.dmoz.org)

Once you've selected a search engine or subject directory and keyed in your search terms, the indicated sources will most likely fall into one of two **domain categories**. These are important to know because knowing the type of site it is can help you evaluate its potential usefulness, credibility, even its bias.

The three "Open Domains" place no restrictions on who may register under these domains:

> *.com* designates the site of a commercial business. At some level, the site exists to make a profit, not merely to provide information. Keep this in mind when evaluating, especially for bias.

> *.net* specifies an information network. You should consider a .net site to be a commercial site.

> *.org* signifies a nonprofit organization. Be prepared for the information to reflect the organization's acknowledged (and often unacknowledged) biases. For example, the National Rifle Association is firmly and publicly opposed to most forms of gun control legislation, while Mothers Against Drunk Driving supports imposing severe sentences on drivers who injure others while intoxicated. While .org may provide some of the most recent and well-cited information, the fact that this information is presented to you by an organization with an agenda should certainly make you aware of bias.

One problem with the *.com, .net*, and *.org* domains is that any type of information can be found at these sites. Most personal blogs are in the *.com* and *.net* domains, and just about *any* organization can apply for, and be granted, a *.org* domain, even if the organization's sole purpose is to propagandize its view and advance its agenda.

Then, there are the restricted domains:

> *.edu* designates a degree-granting institution of higher education that is accredited by one of the six U.S. regional accrediting agencies. This includes community colleges.

> *.mil* is restricted to the military of the United States of America.

> *.gov* specifies the site of an agency of the federal government of the United States of America.

> *.int* is the domain of international organizations like NATO (North Atlantic Treaty Organization).

The restrictions regarding *who* can post information on these domains eliminates many of the concerns you should have regarding accuracy in non-restricted domains. But you must always be wary of bias; *every* organization—public, private, local, or international—wants to present information that *supports its own goals.*

For example, former Vice President Al Gore presents a lot of good science in his film on global warming. He also presents some politics in the guise of science. Your job as researcher is to be able to recognize which is which and to know how to deal with it.

We've already looked at some of Ella's preliminary Internet search, but now that she is fully engaged in locating information, she logs into a typical search engine and keys in "Jamestown colony" as her first search term. Over a dozen pages of results turn up, sorted by relevance. Let's take a look at the results of her search.

Search Results for Jamestown Colony Results **1–7** of about **227,500**

1. <u>**Jamestown**,Virginia—Wikipedia, the free encyclopedia</u>
   Guide to **Jamestown**,Virginia, the first permanent
   settlement in America…Throughout the 17th
   was the capital of the Virginia…
   en.wikipedia.org/wiki/**Jamestown**,_Virg

Wikipedia can be very useful when you're choosing and narrowing your topic. Because entries are not always written by experts, however, some teachers will not allow you to use it as a source.

2. <u>**Jamestown**: History of a Colony</u>
   … arrived at **Jamestown** Island. Their goal w
   colony for the … early settlers at **Jamestow**
   threatened the survival of the **colony** and .
   www.amsocamhis.org/jamestown/history/i

This site looks promising to Ella— but she'll have to decide whether it's credible or not.

3. <u>**Jamestown** at 400! 1607–2007</u>
   A celebration of the 400th anniversary of **Jamestown** . . .
   Jamestown was the first English **colony** in North America. An
   historic opportunity to visit historic Virginia . . .
   www.celebrate**jamestown**va.com/1607_2007/index.html

4. <u>**Jamestown**—Octogenica Online Encyclopedia</u>
   . . . encyclopedia article on **Jamestown**. First per
   established by England . . . the **colony** at Jame
   as a commercial venture by . . .
   www.octogenica.com/eb/article-16747698/**J**

   "Dot com" sites are not always good sources, but Ella has heard of this encyclopedia.

5. <u>**Jamestown**, Virginia Genealogical Society</u>
   . . . The society searches records to trace the names of living
   descendants of the **Jamestown** settlers who . . . ancestors among the
   first to arrive at the **colony** in the seventeenth . . .
   www.jamestowngensociety.org/home.htm

6. Adventures in History: **Jamestown**
   Virtual history curricula suitable for grades 3 through 8 focusing on
   colonial Jamestown . . . students can land at the **colony** with Captain
   John Smith and experience . . .
   www.coursesinushistoryk12.com/**jamestown**/index.html

7. Lecture Notes: **Jamestown**
   Hist203 U.S. History to 1865 Prof. Guidalarche
   at **Jamestown** was established . . . Timeline: 16
   1612 1614 1619 1620 . . .
   www.univwri.edu/dept_hist/hist203/guidalarc

   The ".edu" suffix catches Ella's eye, but this site doesn't look very useful.

Ella immediately notices Wikipedia and Encyclopedia Octogenica on the list, but she doesn't click on these links—she's already got enough general information. She also decides to skip the two "dot com" sites. The first seems to be aimed at tourists, and the second is a site that sells books and other materials to schools.

One of the big advantages of Internet research is how quickly and easily you can check out a potential source. By clicking on the other links, Ella quickly rules out the Jamestown Genealogical Society (not really relevant) and the Lecture Notes (too hard to use). She decides that the web article "Jamestown: History of a Colony" is credible and relevant enough to use in her paper. With just a few keystrokes and mouse-clicks, Ella's found another source! Next, she'll try new search terms, such as "Jamestown economy" and "Jamestown as model colony."

> As powerful and helpful as the Internet is, however, it still does not provide access to 100% of the information you will find helpful in learning about your topic and collecting information to support your thesis. The **library** is still an invaluable collection of material—both print and non-print.
>
> Remember, for an out-of-print, public domain book to be available from sites like Gutenberg.org and Bartleby.com, someone had to key it in. While volunteers for both organizations are busily keying in new material all the time, there are still thousands of books available only in print or manuscript form, and this does not include the enormous number of out-of-print books that are still protected by copyright and *cannot* be made available online.
>
> Sites like Amazon.com and Borders.com can tell you that a book exists, and they may help you contact a seller so you can buy these hard-to-find books, but they are commercial sites, and you must *purchase* the books. The library allows you to borrow the book free of charge—or sit and use it, even if you can't remove it from the library.
>
> The same is true of other print materials like magazines and newspapers, many of which are available online, but many of which are not. Also, some of these print sources do not make *all* of their content available online, and much of what is available *is* so for a cost.

The library is also still an excellent source of CDs and DVDs, which may or may not be available online, but are usually for purchase, and not for cost-free, short-term use.

Furthermore, the reference librarian is a wealth of information and can steer you to the best sources of information for your particular topic. This person can be tremendously useful, so don't feel you have to root aimlessly through hundreds of books to find what you need—just ask!

The bottom line is, you are not going to be able to say you've done a thorough search for the best sources available without making a few trips to one or more libraries.

Let's join **Ella** at her town's public library. At first, she's not sure how to search the library's extensive collections of books, periodicals, reference materials, CD-ROMs, and so on. Like most libraries, Ella's local library's catalog is computerized. A librarian leads Ella to a computer dedicated to a database of the library's holdings, and shows her how to enter terms to search by author, title, subject, or keyword—not very different from conducting a search for information on the Internet.

At first, Ella tries using "Jamestown" as a keyword search term. She gets nearly a hundred hits, but many are irrelevant, such as books about other cities called Jamestown. So, she narrows the search by adding "colonial" to "Jamestown." Take a look at what Ella finds.

The information you will find in your keyword search might not be formatted in exactly the same way as the following table, but every library's system will yield essentially the same information about the sources available in its collection. All items are invented, except "Jamestown: A Beginning" which should be in the public domain because it is a government document.

Basic Keyword Search: Jamestown + colonial   Items 1-7 **Next** ==>

Item	Author	Title	Format	Year	Call Number/Status
1*	Gallant, Edward J.	Colonial Jamestown: A History for Young Readers	Book	2000	F234.J3 G496 2000—AVAILABLE
2*	Pollock, Benjamin	The Life of John Smith	Book	1978	F234.J3 P24 1978—DUE 10/3
3*		Dictionary of American Historical Biography, vol1: 1600-1700	Reference	1988	REF: E129.675 F627 1988
4*	Anderton, R. Keltho, ed.	Jamestown: Four Centuries of History	Book	2007	F234.J3 A523 2007—AVAILABLE
5*	Abnigail, Frances	Black, White, and Red: Racial Conflict in America's First Colony	Book	1996	F234.J34 A26 1996—AVAILABLE
6*	Townshed, Jonathan	Economic Perspectives on Colonial America: Jamestown	Microform	2002	MIC: 12476
7*	U.S. Dept. of Interior	Jamestown: A Beginning	Government Publication	1980	GOV: I 29.2:J 23/2

> **Item 2**: Ella thinks this book would be very useful, but it's checked out. She'll have to come back.

> **Item 3**: Reference books like this one offer concise, credible overviews. Ella can find this book in her library's reference department.

> **Item 4**: The "ed." after the name R. Keltho Anderton means that Anderton is the editor. Most likely, this book collects articles by other authors.

> **Item 6**: Don't be frightened by strange formats. Ella's never used microforms before, but for this source she'll learn—it looks great!

> **Item 7**: Libraries often keep government documents and publications like this one in special sections.

As you can see, the library has some good sources for Ella! *Jamestown: Four Centuries of History; Economic Perspectives on Colonial America: Jamestown; and Jamestown: A Beginning* are all promising. Ella decides she'll bypass *Colonial Jamestown: A History for Young Readers* and *Black, White,* and *Red: Racial Conflict in America's First Colony*—the first is probably written at too low a level, and the second sounds very contentious but not very relevant. She'll come back for the biography, *The Life of John Smith,* when it's returned to the library.

> Don't ignore the wealth of information available from **museums** and **reconstructions**. What you can learn about the artist you're researching by viewing his or her artwork in person cannot be replicated by any number of reproductions of the same work. To stand beside the reconstructed bones of an extinct dinosaur gives you a much clearer sense of the animal's size than any description and illustration can. If at all possible, Ella should make at least one visit to Jamestown, Virginia, and talk to the docents and on-site archaeologists and historians. The student writing about Gothic architecture should visit the nearest cathedral, and so on. If you continue on to college and graduate school, you'll find these research trips are not only "advisable," but absolutely necessary.

> **Talking to the expert(s)** is another invaluable means of collecting information. This is made all the easier by e-mail, instant messaging, and improved telecommunications so that you can speak to someone on the other side of the globe for little more than the cost of a local phone call. You do want to make sure, however, that, before you ask an expert to give up his or her time to help you, you *fully prepare* yourself with prior knowledge of your topic and appropriate questions to make sure you get the information you need. You do not want your contact with the expert to be the *very beginning* of your research.

EXERCISE EIGHT:

GATHERING ADDITIONAL SOURCES

Now, apply to your own research assignment what you have learned.

Add to the list of the sources you began to collect in Exercise Three. Examine each source to determine its usefulness. Make certain you have *several* potential sources from both the Internet and at least one library. Make certain you also have *at least one* museum-type source and/or expert to contact.

Internet Sources:

Write down the bibliographical information for this source.

What type of domain is this source (.com, .org, etc.)?

How might the domain affect the source's usefulness?

How likely are you to use this source? Why?

Library Sources:

Write down the bibliographical information for this source.

What type of source is this (book, periodical, CD)?

Is this source currently available?

How likely are you to use this source? Why?

Museum and/or Expert Sources:

Write down the bibliographical information for this source (NOTE: Models for citing this type of source are available on page 200).

How accessible is this source?

How likely are you to use this source? Why?

12. What kinds of sources do I not need?

As you've probably gathered, one of the biggest challenges in the hunt for *good* sources is avoiding *bad* sources. You know that the sources you want are **relevant**—they contain information about your topic and your thesis. You also know that good sources are **credible**—reliable and worthy of your readers' trust, as well as your own.

You've had a chance to practice evaluating both relevance and credibility and finding the kinds of sources you need.

What about *bad* sources—the kinds you *don't* need? If you keep in mind our original definition of a research paper—**a thesis-driven essay**—and focus on your purpose—**to support [your] ideas and arguments**—it should not be difficult to realize what types of sources you do not need to bother looking at.

Electronic Sources:

> Personal web pages, such as blogs and social networking sites;

> Sites blatantly promoting political or other agendas—especially those that seem extremely to the left or to the right;

> Public message boards where *anyone* can post *anything*, especially those forums that require no form of identification and no sense of a poster's credentials;

> Blatantly commercial sites, especially those for overly avant-garde products or services;

> Any site that has not been updated in over a year.

Non-print Sources:

> Purely fictional television shows, movies, and plays *unless* you are using them for primary source material;

> CDs, DVDs, tapes, records, etc., that were produced for purely commercial or entertainment purposes, again, *unless* you are using them for primary source material;

> Amateur reenactments or reconstructions not affiliated with a recognized and reputable historical or academic organization.

Print Sources:

> Supermarket-style tabloid newspapers and magazines, *unless* you are using them for primary source material;

> Popular, commercial periodicals aimed at a particular demographic (again, *unless* you are using them for primary source material);

> Mass-market, general knowledge encyclopedias, abridgements, and compilations;

> Abridgements, condensations, or "language-adapted" works of literature (NOTE: here we are talking about things like "modernizations" of Shakespeare's language, not translations of works from foreign languages into English);

> Oversimplifications and overgeneralizations (e.g. _____ *for Dummies*, _____ *Made Easy*, etc.)

We've seen how Ella is deciding what sources she needs, but how is she figuring out which sources she *doesn't* need? Ella's teacher helps by steering the entire class away from the popular and free Internet encyclopedias that allow unknown authors to provide information without a standard vetting process. While the entries on such sites are informative, and the serious contributors occasionally question the accuracy, objectivity, and validity of the information, Ella has reached the stage in her research when she needs more in-depth and verifiable information than such sources provide.

Of course, that leaves Ella many, many more sources to sort through. Watch as she examines four potential sources and see why they don't make the cut.

> At the library, Ella takes a look on the shelves for *Colonial Jamestown: A History for Young Readers*. It's published by a reputable educational publisher, and the author is a history professor. Ella sits down to skim the short book.

Jamestown was the first English colony in North America to last. Other settlers tried, but failed. Jamestown faced many difficulties. Many settlers died. Some kept diaries. Those diaries told of those difficulties and how the settlers found ways to get by. The hardships included disease, war with local tribes, and disagreement among settlers. Yet the colony survived.

Because this book is written for "young readers," Ella decides that it will not help her. The information will most likely be too general and presented in only the simplest terms. It probably won't even approach the economic and commercial aspects of the colony that Ella needs to research in depth.

> While she's at the library, another source Ella decides to take a look at is an article titled "Unearthing Jamestown." The article was written by an award-winning journalist, who has traveled the world researching her stories. It appears in a 1973 issue of *American Readers* magazine.

Archaeologists found evidence of extensive use of local natural resources, in addition to tools and materials that the settlers brought with them. Kitchen utensils, work tools, and weapons tended to be mostly of the imported variety, while building materials, fencing, and fasteners were crafted from local timber and stone. The team was disappointed to find little evidence that Native American technology might have influenced the settlers in terms of how they built their first settlement or used the land they claimed.

Ella rules this article out, as well. First of all, she decides it is irrelevant. Secondly, being aimed at a popular audience, the information in the article is likely to be too general for Ella's research purposes. Finally, because it was published in 1973, Ella doesn't want to take a chance on a source that could present information that might be obsolete. If the archaeological project at Jamestown has continued, what might they have discovered since this article was written at the very beginning of the project?

> Of course, Ella is doing some of her research on the Internet—where she will find countless sources that won't help at all.

One site her search engine found was "Survival at Jamestown." Ella clicked on **www.bloggnation.com/HistoryBuffBarry/SurvivalatJamestown.htm,** * and here's a bit of what she found.

If you think about how terrible life must have been for those poor settlers (after all, by the end of that first awful winter, over a third of the settlers had died horrible deaths from disease, malnutrition, execution for treason against leaders, and bloody, vicious Indian ambushes), it seems incredibly greedy of the Virginia Company to have worried only about a profitable return on their financial investment. The people were carving out a new nation, for Pete's sake! And they had more important problems than shipping back furs and precious metals to their penny-pinching investors!

Ella quickly decides that this site, being a blog, is not credible, too heavily opinionated, and not overly concerned with facts to support the opinion. "Barry" might be a true history scholar, but we have no information about him and his sources. Furthermore, the author seems to be biased against the Virginia Company that funded the colony. Ella doesn't bookmark this site.

Another website the search engine turns up is titled "The Shocking Truth About Jamestown." The URL—

www.historyview.net/americancolonies/Jamestown/shockingtruth.html

—immediately looks suspicious. Nonetheless Ella clicks on it and finds the following:

> Everyone knows the story of John Smith and pocahontas and everyone knows about Pocahonta's later marrage to John Rolfe, few historians are willing to admit the lurid affair the Indian princess had with the first Captain of the Colony and the illegitimate child she bore him...

Ella immediately leaves this site. The spelling and grammatical errors are indications that the site is not one she could use. It reads like a supermarket tabloid, and there is nothing to establish the credibility of the site or its anonymous author.

By being careful, Ella has ruled out four sources that would have weakened her research paper. When you do your own research, try to be as skeptical as Ella. After all, your credibility (and your grade) will be at stake.

EXERCISE NINE:

PRACTICING EVALUATING POTENTIAL SOURCES

Examine the following sources and help Rob decide whether the potential sources he is considering will be useful to him.

Rob

Focused Topic: How the development of the railroads increased the movement west and changed the nature of those who went.

Preliminary Thesis: Without the construction of the Transcontinental Railroad in 1869, the United States of America could quite possibly have developed east-west differences even more significant than those that divided the northern and southern states.

Source 1: A discussion forum on issues in United States history:

> http://delaware.speakout.org/forums/?forumID=15*

---

xrp **Why is called "Transcontinental?"** < Mrkie > 04/29/08 11:11

>Why is the Transcontinental Railroad called "Transcontinental" when it doesn't cross the entire continent?

sca **Only from Mississippi** < bgdawg > 04/29/08 11:12

>Your right. It only starts in Mississippi.

efn **Kansas** < justie > 04/29/08 11:12

>>It started in Kansas.

Utah, idiots! < TBB > 04/29/08 11:14

>>I just studied this in school. It started at Provost, Utah.

That was western line!!!!!< MgMgMM > 04/29/08   11:15

>>The WESTERN half ENDED in PROMONTOTY SUMMIT, Utah.

sca **Eastern started at Golden Gate** < jumpinjax > 04/29/08 11:17

>>That's right, Mg, the eastern part started at the famous Golden Gate.

THANK YOU! < MgMgMM > 04/29/08 11:31

>>Finally, someone who knows something!.

So why is it called "Transcontinental?"< Mrkie > 04/29/08 11: 33

>>But why is it called "Transcontinental" when it doesn't cross the entire continent?

Will this source be useful?

Why or why not?

Source 2: Print publication: "Golden Spike Found! Heiress Turns Historical Object into Bracelet." *Weekly News of the World* 26 May 2008: 17.*

"Legend has it that the notorious Golden Spike, driven into the ground on May 10, 1869, in Promontory Summit, Utah, at the completion of the first North American Transcontinental Railroad, was stolen within *minutes* of the end of the ceremony and has never been found. Now, sources close to Molly Bachsgar, heiress to the Ameri-Tram Railroad fortune, have revealed that the spike, estimated to be worth millions of dollars, was actually 'stolen' by a trusted family servant and has never left the family vault! Not until Ms. Bachsgar decided last week to wear the historical object to her brother's engagement party. Ms. Bachsgar, who has been hospitalized with an undisclosed shoulder injury since her brother's party, was unavailable for comment..."

Will this source be useful?

Why or why not?

EXERCISE TEN:

EVALUATING YOUR OWN SOURCES

Now, apply to your own research assignment what you have learned.

Look over your list of sources and examine each, this time with an eye toward eliminating bad or useless sources.

Source 1:

Write down the bibliographical information for this source.

Why have you chosen to exclude this source?

13. How do I keep track of the sources I've found?

So far, we've spent the bulk of our time and energy finding and evaluating potential sources. The reason for that should be fairly obvious: without enough information, you cannot write your paper. Without *good* information from reliable sources, you'll never be able to support your thesis.

How many sources *are* enough? There's no way to answer that question. Your teacher will probably impose a minimum expectation (for example, no fewer than five sources of varied types), but that is only to help you learn that copying out of a single book, or cutting and pasting from a couple of websites is not research—in fact, it's plagiarism, and we'll deal with that a lot in later pages.

Again, how many sources are enough? You'll know you have enough sources when you finish writing your paper, and you feel good that you've made the best case you can for your thesis.

Having *enough* sources, however, and gathering *enough* information, as you've learned, are not the problems. At some point you need to keep track of your sources and the information you get from each.

In Chapter 2, we listed "Organizing Sources" as the second major step of the research process. As books, articles, and website bookmarks and printouts begin to form little mountains in your work area, you can fight the chaos with some basic organization strategies. It's helpful to start organizing **while you're hunting**, instead of trying to bring order to your sources after the fact (sort of like putting your clothes away as you're done with them, rather than letting everything pile up and trying to clean your room once a month).

There is no one specific way to organize your sources, but that does not excuse you from having to experiment with different organizational strategies and finding what works for you. Probably the two most likely organizational patterns, however, would be by usefulness and by sub-topic.

> **By importance or usefulness**: You've already spent a good deal of time evaluating your potential sources for their credibility, relevance, and overall usefulness. Chances are you'll want to examine the sources you think will be most useful first, saving those you have doubts about for later—if you end up needing them at all.

> **By topic**: Of course, you have only one topic. As you've no doubt seen, a thorough discussion of your main topic will require your exploring a number of different aspects, elements, and issues of that topic. For example, Ella's research into the relationship between the Plymouth settlers and the Massachusetts protesters one hundred and fifty years later has already taken her into some study of the English Separatist Movement, the politics and theology of seventeenth-century England, the economics of founding a colony, and so forth. Of course, at some point Ella will want to formalize these sub-topics into an outline to organize her paper, but for the time being, as long as she can organize her sources to predict what information she's likely to get from which source, she'll be ahead of the game.

Here are several of the sources Ella has gathered so far, along with her own notes, descriptions of the sources, and some actual quotations. Watch how Ella sorts these sources into highly useable, barely useable (low), or somewhere in the middle.

Highly Useable:

> *The Virtual Jamestown Archive*. 15 December 2001. Virginia Polytechnic Institute and State University, the University of Virginia, and the Virginia Center for Digital History. 22 April 2008 < http:// www.virtualjamestown.org>. "Includes maps, labor contracts, public records, *firsthand accounts and letters…"…probably some useful primary source material here…a collaboration between two good Virginia schools…information should be reliable and credible.*

> *Colonists and Native Americans*. 01 June 1998. A part of the Texts and Documents project at Hanover College. 22 April 2008 <http://history.hanover.edu/project.html#17>.*

> "The Colonial Library." *A Compendium of Primary Source Documents*. 08 August 2007. Dr. Richard Gander. 30 April 2008 <http://home. wi.rr.com/rickgander/primarysources.htm>.* "historical documents and archival information" *…might find some primary source material here. Site is maintained by a respectable college…credible and reliable.*

Ella knows that primary source material is very important for a research paper. She places any source that might yield this material in her "top" range.

> *The Life of John Smith.* Los Angeles: POD Press, 1978.*
...primary source by Smith himself...

> Abnigail, Frances. *Black, White, and Red: Racial Conflict in America's first Colony.* Newark, NJ: Seminole Publishers, 1996.*
"...explores in some depth how racial tensions and demographic instability threatened to destroy the fledgling settlement and how those difficulties were ultimately overcome..."

The *Smith* book is, again, a potentially helpful primary source, and the historians' commentary will probably yield some important insights. The Abnigail book seems perfect for Ella's paper about how changes in this first colony—probably including demographic changes—influenced the establishment and nature of subsequent colonies.

> Goddard, Woodward, Ph. D. *Economics of Early North American Settlements.* Princeton, NJ: Princeton University Press, 2005.*

Since the Plantation was first intended to be a commercial enterprise, and I know really very little about how investment companies worked, this book might be very helpful.

This final book looks as if it will have a *lot* of good information.

The Middle Ground:

> Anderton, R. Keltho, ed. *Jamestown: Four Centuries of History.* Norfolk, VA: Patriot Press, 2007.*

Will probably provide a decent overview, but is more of a "pop-culture" book than an in-depth history.

> *Seekers of Truth in History.* 01 April 1984. Americans for Truth, Justice, and the American Way. 05 May 2008 <http://www.truthhistory.org.>*

"Perhaps the hardest lesson we learn **by examining both sides** is that the heroes of history were…mere human beings living the best they knew how,…James I abhorred…tobacco, but it kept his colony alive and made him rich."

"…in 1612, no one knew of addiction and health risks associated with tobacco smoke or…'dipping' snuff."

"The fact of the matter is that none of the good the United States has brought to the world would have been possible without the bad."

Seems balanced, thoughtful. Really seeks to look at "both sides."

> *The United States and Moral Compromise.* 23 March 2001. No affiliated organization or institution cited. 41 April 2008 <http://www.morallycompromised.com>.*

"The seeds of America's damnation were first sown in 1612…"

"…tobacco was a profane and pagan plant with which the savage population of the Americas seduced their European liberators…"

"So wealthy had the avaricious colonists become that they were able to afford an import that would assure the country's doom."

Wow, completely one-sided and blatantly biased toward a "damned America" point of view. Still, some of the "evidence" might be factual.

As we've already discussed, blatantly biased sources are usable but do present some problems that must be dealt with in the paper. The Anderton book, if it is too much like a tourist souvenir, might end up in the bottom tier.

Barely Useable:

> Gallant, Edward J. *Colonial Jamestown: A History for Young Readers.* New York: Seagull Group, 2000.*
For readers under the age of 12. Not loaded with information.

> *Jamestown Settlement, living-history museum of early America.* 22 January 2000. <http://www.historyisfun.org/Jamestown-Settlement.htm>.
Seems to be sort of an online, virtual museum, very touristy, fairly basic (tertiary) information, geared mostly for children.

> Pollock, Benjamin. *Dictionary of American Historical Biography, vol. 1: 1600-1700.* New York: Lerner's Media, 1988.*
Short entries. Only secondary sources cited. I think I can do better research.

Anything that is too general or non-specific will not be very helpful to Ella. She is not looking merely to report on others' findings but to argue her own point, her thesis.

Now, let's see how Ella might organize these same sources *if she chose to organize them according to subject.* Notice that, if one source seems to promise information on more than one aspect of her subject, Ella lists the source more than once.

Daily life:

> Gallant, Edward J. *Colonial Jamestown: A History for Young Readers.* New York: Seagull Group, 2000.*

> *Jamestown Settlement, living-history museum of early America.* 22 January 2000. Jamestown-Yorktown Foundation, an agency of the Commonwealth of Virginia that is accredited by the American Association of Museums. 05 May 2008 <http://www.historyisfun. org/Jamestown-Settlement.htm>.

> Anderton, R. Keltho, ed. *Jamestown: Four Centuries of History.* Norfolk, VA: Patriot Press, 2007.*

Struggle to Survive:

> *The Virtual Jamestown Archive.* 15 December 2001. Virginia Polytechnic Institute and State University, the University of Virginia, and the Virginia Center for Digital History. 22 April 2008 < http:// www.virtualjamestown.org>.

> "The Colonial Library." *A Compendium of Primary Source Documents.* 08 August 2007. Dr. Richard Gander. 30 April 2008 <http://home. wi.rr.com/rickgander/primarysources.htm>.*

> *Seekers of Truth in History.* 01 April 1984. Americans for Truth, Justice, and the American Way. 05 May 2008 <http://www.truthhistory. org>.*

> Anderton, R. Keltho, ed. *Jamestown: Four Centuries of History.* Norfolk, VA: Patriot Press, 2007.*

Biographical Information:

> *The Life of John Smith.* Los Angeles: POD Press, 1978.*

> Pollock, Benjamin. *Dictionary of American Historical Biography*, vol1: 1600-1700. New York: Lerner's Media, 1988.*

Domestic and Foreign Relations:

> *Colonists and Native Americans.* 01 June 1998. A part of the Texts and Documents project at Hanover College. 22 April 2008 <http://history.hanover.edu/project.html#17>.*

> Abnigail, Frances. *Black, White, and Red: Racial Conflict in America's first Colony.* Newark, NJ: Seminole Publishers, 1996.*

Commerce/Tobacco Trade:

> Goddard, Woodward, Ph. D. *Economics of Early North American Settlements.* Princeton, NJ: Princeton University Press, 2005.*

> *Seekers of Truth in History.* 01 April 1984. Americans for Truth, Justice, and the American Way. 05 May 2008 < http://www.truthhistory.org>.*

> *The United States and Moral Compromise.* 23 March 2001. No affiliated organization or institution cited. 41 April 2008 <http://www.morallycompromised.com>.*

Notice, also, that while Ella's preliminary thesis governed the search terms she used and the sources she sought, the initial information she is gleaning from those sources is beginning to govern the development of something like an outline. We will discuss outlining in greater detail later.

EXERCISE ELEVEN:

PRACTICING ORGANIZING SOURCES

Now, let's look at the sources Rob has gathered so far. All notes, comments, and descriptions for each source have been reproduced for you. Organize these potential sources, first according to their usefulness, and then according to topic. NOTE that you will have to decide what relevant sub-topics are suggested by the sources and the information they contain.

All of the items that follow are sources you have already dealt with. You have seen descriptions, reviews, and advertising blurbs for all of them. You might find it helpful, however, to review the information you have about each source as you develop an organizational plan.

Rob

Focused Topic: How the development of the railroads increased the movement west and changed the nature of those who went.

Preliminary Thesis: Without the construction of the Transcontinental Railroad in 1869, the United States of America could quite possibly have developed east-west differences even more significant than those that divided the northern and southern states.

Sources:

National Public Radio Broadcast: Experiencing America.
    <http://www.npr.org/klbj/exam/rbeature/rb_interview.html.>*

First North American Transcontinental Railroad Photographic Virtual
    Museum: "A Tribute to the Contributions of Chinese-American to
    the First North American Transcontinental Railroad"
    <http://cprr.org/Museum/Chinese.html>.*

Poole, Victor H. *The Tenuous Relationship between the Government of the United States of America and the Railroads of the Pacific States.* New York: Greene and Greyhound, 1871.*

Prescott, Ansun. ed. *There Went the Neighborhood: The Collected Diaries of Marjorie Holmestead 1850 - 1900 .* San Francisco: Books by the Bay, Inc., 2005.*

The History of United States Imperialism: 1803 - 1898. 01 February 2002. The Buckworthy Institute. 11 May 2008 <http://www.buckworthyinstitute.org>.*

Divergent Views of American History. 10 October 1998. Department of Alternative Studies, University of Saint Michaels. 15 May 2008 <http://www.stmichaelsme.edu/altstu/amhist>.*

Cho, Raymond. *The Noble Chinese and the American Nation.* San Francisco: Allworld Press, 1985.*

http://delaware.speakout.org/forums/?forumID=15*

"Golden Spike Found! Heiress Turns Historical Object into Bracelet." Weekly News of the World 26 May 2008: 17.*

Organize Rob's sources from most useful (1) to least (9). Explain why you have placed the sources in the order you have.

> *NOTE:* For all students' sources, answers will vary, but all organizational patterns must be based on the principles of relevance, credibility, and usability covered so far.

1.

Why the top?:

2.

Why:

3.

Why:

4.

Why only near the middle?:

5.

Why:

6.

Why:

7.

Why:

8.

Why:

9.

Why the bottom?:

Now, list the sub-topics suggested by Rob's sources, and indicate which sources are likely to provide information on that sub-topic.

Sub-topic 1:

Source:

Source:

Source:

Sub-topic 2:

Source:

Source:

Source:

Sub-topic 3:

Source:

Source:

Source:

Sub-topic 4:

Source:

Source:

Source:

Sub-topic 5:

Source:

Source:

Source:

EXERCISE TWELVE:

ORGANIZING YOUR SOURCES

Now, apply to your own research assignment what you have learned.

1. *Review your sources and organize them in order from most useful to least useful. For each, explain why you have placed it where you have, especially explaining why you have selected your top and bottom sources.*

2. *List the sub-topics suggested by your sources, and then indicate which sources are likely to provide information on that sub-topic.*

14. What is a preliminary outline, and when should I draft mine?

Obviously, if it wasn't time to begin to plan your systematic search for information, the question of your Preliminary Outline would not have come up. If you think logically, however, now is the transition between searching for *sources* and searching for *information*, and there is really no more logical time than now to plan what information you're going to look for, and what you plan to do with it once you've found it.

Of course, the most famous type of outline is the academic outline with Roman numerals, Arabic numerals, and upper and lower case letters. If you're like most student writers, you probably understand the rules and format of the outline more than its actual use. An outline can be a very useful tool in researching and writing a top-grade paper. Let's briefly review the elements and principles of an outline, and then examine these principles by looking at how an outline operates.

Each level of notation (Roman numeral, upper case letter, Arabic numeral, lower case letter) represents a particular "size" of the idea noted there:

> Roman numerals (I, II, III) are the **main ideas** you want to establish in your essay.

>Upper case letters (A, B, C) are the **sub-points** into which you can divide your main ideas.

> Arabic numerals (1, 2, 3) are **supporting details**.

>Lower case letters (a, b, c) are **discussions and explanations of those details.**

> And so on.

The indentation formula allows you to *see* the relationship between the main ideas, and the various levels of sub-points under each main idea. In this way, an outline lets you *visually* keep track of your ideas and their relationship to each other.

Indentation Formula:

I.

  A.

    1.

      a.

      b.

    2.

      a.

      b.

  B.

    1.

      a.

      b.

    2.

      a.

      b.

II.

  A.

    1.

      a.

      b.

    2.

      a.

      b.

  B.

    1.

      a.

      b.

    2.

      a.

      b.

Look at how Ella begins to approach her research topic: Jamestown's role as a model for future English settlements in North America. Think about main ideas that need to be addressed as she argues her thesis: *Changes in the management of the Jamestown settlement helped define the nature of future British colonies in North America and eventually the United States.*

Notice that some of her main ideas begin as questions she intends to answer with her research.

> original purpose of/reason for Jamestown settlement

> demographic of original settlers

> early successes or failures

> How was the colony saved?

> What lessons had been learned from the near-failure of the colony?

Now, let's see how she begins to anticipate the information she will need from her sources to discuss those main ideas.

Remember, at this point, that Ella does not necessarily know *what* information she will get from *which* source; she simply knows that she intends to find this information, and she is fairly confident that she either has the sources that will help her, or she can find them.

I. Original purpose of/reason for Jamestown settlement

    – English prestige among other colonizing nations?

    – James I's desire for an empire?

    – Commercial and investment opportunities?

    – Why did the settlers themselves want to come?

Some of this information Ella already knows from her brief reading of the sources she already has.

II. Demographic of original settlers

- How many men?

- What social classes and trades represented?

- How many women?

- What social classes were represented?

- How were original settlers recruited?

III. Early successes or failures

- Relations with Native Americans

- Securing food, drinking water, shelter…

Because she is building a *preliminary outline*, Ella knows that individual items and lines of inquiry can change, but she does lay out for herself as *concrete* a plan as possible.

- Death rate/survival rate?

- Fulfilling original intent of the colony

IV. How was the colony saved?

- Sending additional settlers and provisions

Notice that there really is no hard information in this outline. That's because Ella has not done her research yet. The purpose of this outline is to establish a "shopping list" of what she intends to find and present.

- Change in government?

- Change in colonial economy?

- Change in philosophy/intent of colony?

V. What lessons had been learned from the near-failure of the colony?

  - Lessons about the reason for settlement

  - About the settlers

  - About the government and economy of the settlement

  - Other

Now, let's watch as she begins to anticipate the information she will need from her sources to discuss those sub-points.

Remember that, at this point, Ella does not necessarily know *what* information she will get from *which* source; she does know that she intends to find this information, and she is fairly confident that she either has the sources that will help her, or she can find them.

I. Original purpose of/reason for Jamestown settlement

  A. English prestige among other colonizing nations?

  A. James I's desire for an empire?

    - English prestige among other colonizing nations

Notice that Ella has decided to change what she originally thought was going to be a main idea into a sub-point.

    - Increase royal treasury

Again, early notes from one of Ella's sources mentioned the wealth James amassed from the tobacco trade. This brief note suggests to Ella that she should explore a desire for wealth as a reason for wanting an Empire.

B. Commercial and investment opportunities?

- the formation of the Virginia Company

- the thing about furs, precious metals, and a trade route with the East

C. Why did the settlers themselves want to come?

- personal reasons?

- desire for wealth?

- any notions yet of desire for freedom?

II.   Demographic of original settlers

A. How many men?

B. What social classes and trades represented?

C. How many women?

Ella knows from her preliminary reading that there were no women in the first wave of settlers. In fact, including women among the settlers was one of the changes made in future colonies. Ella also begins to think that, if she cannot think of areas of further development for this section of her outline, perhaps it should not be a separate section but included somewhere else.

D. What social classes were represented?

E. How were original settlers recruited?

III. Early successes or failures

   A. Relations with Native Americans

      - Fear and distrust/attacks on fort

      - Overtures of friendship (?)

   B. Securing food, drinking water, shelter...

      - problems with farming

      - problems with hunting

      - issue with "gentlemen" refusing to work

   C. Death rate/survival rate?

   D. Fulfilling original intent of the colony

      - Did they find precious metals?

      - Did they manage to trap for furs?

      - Was there serious exploration for Northwest Passage?

IV. How was the colony saved?

   A. Sending additional settlers and provisions

      - Who were the new settlers, and how were they recruited?

      - What skills, etc., did these new settlers have?

   B. Change in government?

      - John Smith to John Rolfe?

      - What help (if any) did Smith negotiate for when he returned to England?

Again, Ella would unable to compose this outline with no knowledge. That is why the preliminary outline is written after some initial reading and research.

C. Change in colonial economy?

- Was there early trade? What was initial export?

- Rolfe's (or Smith's) switch to tobacco as a cash crop

D. Change in philosophy/intent of colony?

- from Plantation (for benefit of outside investors) to Colony (for benefit of settlers)

Ella knows she cannot have only one point of development, so if this is the only change she knows to explore, she will have to restructure this part of her discussion.

V. What lessons had been learned from the near-failure of the colony?

A. Lessons about the reason for settlement

- from Plantation to Colony

- based on colonists desires and needs (e.g., Plymouth)

B. About the settlers

- include women

- workers and merchants, not "gentlemen"

- stronger motivation to succeed than mere profit

C. About the government and economy of the settlement.

- internal, democratic government rather than externally-imposed

- self-sustaining

- profit benefits settlers and colony, not outside investors

D. Other

Having watched Ella develop her preliminary outline, let's review some of the conventions of the academic outline and examine how and why they came about:

You cannot have only one item at a particular level. Think of it this way:

> If your Roman numerals are the main "parts" of your topic,

> and the upper case letters are the "parts" of the Roman numeral under which you've placed them,

> and the Arabic numerals are "parts" of the upper case letters, and so on...

...then remember that *you cannot break something into only one part!* Therefore, for every "**I**" you need a "**II**;" for every "**A**" you need a "**B**;" for every "**1**" you need a "**2**;" and so on.

Notice again that, in **IV. D.**, Ella had only one "part" in which to break her main idea, "Change in philosophy/intent of colony." She used the "more than one part" principle to diagnose a potential problem with her plan. It will certainly be easier for her to fix it now than to have to rewrite a flawed paper!

It is also important that you strive to develop every part of your topic to the same level. In outline terms, that means if you go to the lower-case-letter level in one section, you should make a concerted effort to go that deep in all of your sections. By describing one aspect of your topic in full detail and then glossing over another with barely a mention, you'll end up with a very uneven argument that any opposition will easily discredit.

EXERCISE THIRTEEN:

PRACTICING OUTLINING

Now help Rob review the information he has already gathered, think about the points he wants to argue, and draft his preliminary thesis.

Rob

Focused Topic: How the development of the railroads increased the movement west and changed the nature of those who went.

Preliminary Thesis: Without the construction of the Transcontinental Railroad in 1869, the United States of America could quite possibly have developed east-west differences even more significant than those that divided the northern and southern states.

Brainstorm the main ideas that Rob will most likely need to discuss in his paper:

Next, break each of Rob's main ideas into the logical sub-points:

What details, facts, and examples is Rob going to need to fully develop the sub-points of his discussion?:

It's now time to help Rob compose his preliminary outline. Remember to apply the conventions of Roman and Arabic numerals and upper case letters to organize your topics and sub-topics:

EXERCISE FOURTEEN:

DRAFTING YOUR PRELIMINARY OUTLINE

Now, apply to your own research paper what you've learned and practiced.

Focused Topic:

Preliminary Thesis:

What main ideas will you most likely need to discuss in your paper?

Next, break each those main ideas into logical sub-points:

What details, facts, and examples are you going to need to fully develop the sub-points of your discussion?

Now, compose your preliminary outline.

15. How much time will I need for my research?

For most of your school-related research projects, you will be given definitive start and stop dates. For a paper like the one Ella is writing (6–10 pages), you will probably be given no less than a month to six weeks.

The question, then, isn't so much the amount of time you'll need as it is how to budget your time, how not to spend too much time on one step and leave yourself panicked without enough time for a later step.

Earlier, we described each of the steps in the research process. Think logically, and try to arrange the steps below from the least time-consuming (taking, maybe, only a few hours) to the most time-consuming (taking, perhaps, a full week or two). Also, speculate how much time you should allow for each step, assuming your due date is six weeks from now.

Number each step (1 for shortest, two for next shortest, etc.) and estimate the amount of time you think might be appropriate for that step.

1. Selecting and focusing your subject
2. Developing a preliminary thesis
3. Collecting and evaluating potential sources
4. Organizing your sources
5. Drafting your preliminary outline
6. Examining your source material and taking notes
7. Finalizing your thesis
8. Finalizing your outline
9. Writing the first draft of your paper
10. Finalizing your Works Cited Page
11. Revising and editing
12. Writing the final draft of your paper
13. Performing your final proof

Now, compare your estimations with our suggestions:

7. Finalizing your thesis—*less than an hour*

10. Finalizing your Works Cited Page—*one hour or less*

4. Organizing your sources—*one hour or two*

13. Performing your final proof—*an hour or two**

5. Drafting your preliminary outline—*an hour or two*

2. Developing a preliminary thesis—*one day*

11. Revising and editing—*one to one and a half days**

12. Writing the final draft of your paper—*one or two days**

8. Finalizing your outline—*one or two days*

1. Selecting and focusing your subject—*one or two days*

3. Collecting and evaluating potential sources—*two or three days*

9. Writing the first draft of your paper—*two or three days**

6. Examining your source material and taking notes—*several weeks*

Are there any steps for which you are surprised by our suggestion? Are there any steps for which your estimation and our suggestion vary greatly (by more than a day)? Where? For what steps did you severely overestimate the time? For what steps did you severely underestimate the time?

The point of this exercise is that many students mistakenly believe that the longest and most difficult steps in the process are the drafting and revising steps. As a result, they spend too little time and energy on what should be the *primary steps*, the research itself. If you really interact with your sources, really process the information, the writing of the paper becomes almost a mere formality.

* The time allowed for many of these steps depends, of course, on the length of the paper you are to write. This book is based on the idea that you are writing a six- to ten-page paper. A longer paper will require a longer time to write.

Following our suggestions, and assuming that your teacher has given you six weeks for your research project, you should be given (or should be able to develop) a research schedule similar to the ones below. We've given you two schedules—one for a fall-semester class and one for a spring-semester class:

Deadlines (Spring Semester):

> Monday, April 7th: Topic due (NOTE: This is the day you *have* your topic. The two days thinking of a topic occurred *before* this.

> Wednesday, April 9th: Preliminary thesis due

> Monday, April 14th: Preliminary list of sources and evaluations due (This step also includes organizing your sources to prepare for your research.)

> Tuesday, April 15th: Preliminary outlines due

A little more than a week into your research project, and you're ready to attack your sources and gather information. It is now too late to find out there is not "enough information," for you to completely change your topic.

> Monday, April 28th: Notes due.

> Tuesday, April 29th: Final thesis due.

You've spent two weeks examining your sources and gathering information. You either know the point you are prepared to argue in your paper, or you're in extreme danger.

> Wednesday, April 30th: Final outline due.

> Monday, May 5th: First draft due. (NOTE: This *includes* all citations and Works Cited Page.)

> Monday, May 12th: Final draft due. (NOTE: Between last Monday and today, you've reread your first draft, performed all necessary revising and editing, written the final draft, and performed the final proof.)

Deadlines (Fall Semester):

> Monday, October 6th: Topic due (NOTE: This is the day you *have* your topic. The two days thinking of a topic occurred *before* this.

> Wednesday, October 8th: Preliminary thesis due

> Monday, October 13th : Preliminary list of sources and evaluations due (This step also includes organizing your sources to prepare for your research.)

> Tuesday, October 14th: Preliminary outlines due

A little more than a week into your research project, and you're ready to attack your sources and gather information. It is now too late to find out there is not "enough information," and you need to completely change your topic.

> Monday, October 27th: Notes due.

> Tuesday, October 28th: Final thesis due.

You've spent two weeks examining your sources and gathering information. You either *know* the point you are prepared to argue in your paper or you're in danger.

> Wednesday, October 29th: Final outline due.

> Monday, November 3rd: First draft due. (NOTE: This *includes* all citations and Works Cited Page.)

> Monday, November 10th: Final draft due. (NOTE: Between last Monday and today, you've reread your first draft, performed all necessary revising and editing, written the final draft, and performed the final proof.)

EXERCISE FIFTEEN:

DRAFTING A RESEARCH SCHEDULE

Rob's teacher has assigned his research paper to be due Monday, December 15, providing no other scheduling assistance or interim due dates.

Help Rob plan his research timelines.

EXERCISE SIXTEEN:

DRAFTING YOUR OWN RESEARCH SCHEDULE

Now, apply to your own research project what you've learned and practiced and draft the research schedule you will use for your paper.

Chapter
4

IN THE THICK OF IT

16. What do I do with all of these sources?

You know that they say the best way to take off a band-aid is to rip it off and get it over with in a hurry. They also say the best way to get used to cold water in a pool or lake is to just dive in and get yourself wet.

It's the same with doing your research.

So, gather all of the tools you've assembled: research process timeline (including due dates of preliminary components), preliminary thesis, preliminary outline, prioritized list of potential sources, and dive in. If you need to visit any museums or actual sites, schedule those visits. If you need to interview anyone, make your initial contact and schedule the interviews. (ALWAYS keep in mind that you might want time to do follow-up visits or ask follow-up questions while you are still in the note-taking stage.) Check libraries for the availability of any books or other hard-copy sources (including CDs and DVDs), perhaps even signing them out to use first, while you know that they are available.

As you begin your paper in earnest, this chapter will help you approach your sources, get as much from them as you can, and keep yourself always organized, so that you don't lose sight of the final paper you are eventually going to have to write.

17. How do I take notes on my sources?

Taking notes should not be a new concept to you. Most likely, since elementary school you have been trained to takes notes from what has been written on the board or presented via an overhead projector or computer monitor. You may have been taught and encouraged to take notes during lectures and discussions—being told especially not to try to transcribe every word, but to condense and summarize the gist of the conversation. You've probably even practiced underlining and/or highlighting while reading and jotting notes in the margin of the book you're reading or on separate paper.

One idea that we hope has been well established is that *making a copy of a source is not taking notes*.

Photocopying from a book, printing out a page from an e-mail or the Internet, even hand-copying a paragraph or two from a book, magazine, or newspaper is not note taking.

However, photocopying or hand-copying complete and accurate bibliographical information for every possible entry on your Works Cited Page is absolutely necessary.

For most academic purposes, your notes will take three forms: material *directly from a source* (whether you're quoting, paraphrasing, or summarizing), your *reactions to and discussion of the material* from sources, and your *original ideas*.

You need to have all of these in your paper, and to make sure you do, it's best to have notes on all three.

As Ella watches a *History-Channel*-style DVD on Jamestown, she is learning some good information that she knows she will want to include in her paper. Here are some of her notes:

From: *Jamestown: Fragile Seeds of a Mighty Nation.* Writ. Wilmot
Sneed and Mark Marcke. Dir. Phillip Mayes. The History
Channel. DVD. History Channel Home Video, 2006.*

QT: ANNOUNCER *(check credits for name)*: "The original
settlers were the wrong people, coming to the wrong place,
and for the wrong reason. If there was anything right about the
Virginia Experience, history has not recorded it."

SUM/PPHRASE: *Jamestown: Fragile Seeds*: First "Act" deals with
the Virginia Company and the financial arrangements of the
settlement. Settlers were pretty much indentured servants to the
investors (called "shareholders"). They were to earn their passage
and purchase their freedom by sending home to England fur,
tobacco, and other things that were in short supply there.

QT: *Jamestown: Fragile Seeds*: Professor from Columbia *(check
credits for name)*: "The 'gentlemen' of the settlement were not
settlers at all, but debtors who had been given a choice: prison
in England with no hope ever of buying their way out, or a
speculative journey to the New World that would almost certainly,
all experts agreed, make them enormously wealthy."

ME: *Jamestown: Fragile Seeds*: *My question:* >>Is it any wonder we
evolved into such a materialistic society since, at our very roots,
the United States was little more than an investment, a speculative
venture?<<

SUM/PPHRASE: *Jamestown: Fragile Seeds*: In first Act, we learn that
the settlement's failure to send goods home was not because the
goods were not available, but the settlers, who had no idea how to
survive in the wilderness, were unable to get at them.

ME: *Jamestown: Fragile Seeds*: *It seems to me*: >> future colonies
probably fared better from the beginning because they learned (1)
to send the right people (people who had a real desire to begin
a new life and who were willing to work to build that life), (2)
for the right reason (people who were asking to leave, not being
bribed or threatened).<<

Ella is off to a good start, and she seems to understand how to take notes on material as she reads, listens, or watches. Notice what Ella has done, which is what you need to do, as well, to help guarantee an excellent research paper.

1. Ella clearly identifies the source from which she got this information. She records this *as she takes the note* so that later she will not confuse her sources, fail to credit the correct source, or be accused of plagiarism.

2. Ella has some direct quotations, and she knows she needs to be able to provide an attribution for each quotation in her paper (in addition to the citation and documentation).

3. Ella has both summarized and paraphrased some of the information.

4. Ella is not simply passively taking in information; she is thinking and processing the material she is watching. She also makes a note of questions that occur to her, as well as original ideas.

Believe it or not, Ella's thoughts and questions will be the most important parts of her research paper. If all you do is present information from your sources—even if you organize that research around an argument (your thesis), all you have is a report, not a research paper.

5. Ella has devised a way to visually indicate what is a quotation (underlined, placed in quotation marks, and introduced with *QT*), what is a paraphrase/summary (displayed in plain text and introduced with *SUM/PPHRASE*), and what are her own thoughts (introduced with *ME* and set off in >> <<).

EXERCISE ONE:

EXAMINING RESEARCH NOTES

Now, look at some of the notes Rob has taken for his research paper and offer him constructive criticism on what he's done well and what he needs to do better.

Rob

Focused Topic: How the development of the railroads increased the movement west and changed the nature of those who went.

Preliminary Thesis: Without the construction of the Transcontinental Railroad in 1869, the United States of America could quite possibly have developed east-west differences even more significant than those that divided the northern and southern states.

From: McMahon, Matthew. "How the West was Whipped." *Alt View Quarterly.* Spring 2007: 87-95.*

From "How the West was Whipped":

It makes sense to me that the railroad would have opened the West to women and to men who were not "rough and ready," strong, and adventuresome. After all, a four-day train ride was nothing compared to months on a wagon or the back of a horse. (mine)

From "How the West was Whipped":

p. 95— *"Fred Harvey's dying words to his sons are allegedly, 'Don't cut the ham too thin, boys.'"* He really must have had a reputation for serving a decent meal and not cheating his customers (mine).

From "How the West was Whipped":

//Within a few years of the t.c.r.'s completion, "whistle stop" eating establishments were beginning to open. Hotels too. But the food was lousy and the service even worse. In 1876 (less than 20 years after the tcr), Fred Harvey opened his first Harvey House (Atchison, Topeka, and Santa Fe RR). Harvey girls were highly supervised and brought civilizing influence to the West.//

1. So far, what is Rob doing right?

2. What does Rob need to do better?

EXERCISE TWO:

TAKING NOTES

Now, apply to your own research paper what you've learned and practiced. Record the notes you have taken from one of your sources, keeping in mind that you must have some direct quotations, some summary/paraphrase, and some of your own thoughts.

Remember also that you must be able to credit each bit of information to the correct source and provide attributions for all quotations.

You should also be able to distinguish easily among which notes are directly from your sources and which are your own ideas.

From what source have you taken these notes?

Direct quotations:

Summary/paraphrase:

Original thoughts:

How are you distinguishing among the different types of notes you have taken?

One of the keys to good note taking—and very helpful in avoiding plagiarism, as well as *actually learning* something about your topic—is learning how to paraphrase effectively. It's often been said that, if you cannot explain an idea to someone else *in your own words*, then, you don't really understand the idea.

Paraphrasing makes certain that you *do* understand the ideas you're learning. Taking the ideas and restating them in your own words is also a very effective way to make certain that you'll remember the information even after you've written the paper and turned it in.

Direct quotation is important when you *must* present the material in exactly the same way your source does, and summary is useful in presenting a large block of information, but paraphrase is the most effective means of learning and then demonstrating what you've learned.

Remember, however, that you will still need to cite the source that gave you the information, regardless of whether you paraphrase, summarize, or use direct quotations.

Here's the original text, from Ella's United States history textbook:

> Jamestown was beset by many difficulties as early settlers struggled to tame the land and deal with natives. "Share-holders" funded the venture and remained in England, expecting the settlers—generally poor farmers and tradesmen and their families—to quickly turn a profit from the bounty of natural resources in the "New World."
>
> Early on, however, it was all the settlers could do to keep from starving to death. With no immediate profit to be had, and settlers struggling merely to stay alive, many questioned whether the venture would survive, let alone become a model for many (though not all) future settlements in the region.

And here's Ella's first attempt at a paraphrase:

> *Jamestown was beset by many troubles. Early settlers struggled to tame the land and also deal with the aboriginal natives. The investors, who had funded the venture and remained in England, expected the settlers (who were mostly poor farmers and tradesmen and their families) to make a quick profit from the bountiful natural resources of the "New World."*
>
> *It took all of the settlers' time and energy simply to keep from starving to death. Seeing no immediate profit, and settlers struggling merely to survive, many people questioned whether the venture would survive, let alone become a model for future settlements.*

This is an unacceptable paraphrase and would count as plagiarism!

Ella has only changed around a few words and phrases. The entire passage is still nothing more than her source's words and ideas.

If she is going to use this passage in her paper, she is going to have to cite the source in the body of her paper. (See section 30: "Why, when, and how do I cite my sources?".)

Ella, however, is still early enough in her timeline to show her first notes to her teacher. Being warned that her paraphrase is not sufficient, she tries again:

> *From the beginning, the settlers faced difficulties more severe than they had apparently foreseen. Clearing land for fortification, housing, and farming proved difficult, and early relations with the natives were doubtful, the natives often being hostile to the settlers. The investors, whose sole interest was quick profit from the exploitation of America's abundant natural resources, had stayed in England, so they were not witness to, nor part of, the struggle to survive.*
>
> *When these shareholders realized the possibility of losing their investments and recognized the severe hardship of trying merely to survive, they questioned the advisability of future settlements.*

This paraphrase is acceptable because it accurately conveys the information, largely in Ella's own words. In addition to rephrasing the information from her source, Ella has also chosen words and sentence structures that indicate her understanding of the information she is processing.

Note, however, that Ella should still cite the source of this information in the body of her paper. (See section 30: "Why, when, and how do I cite my sources?")

EXERCISE THREE

EVALUATING PARAPHRASES

Now, look at a few of Rob's attempts to paraphrase passages from his sources. In the spaces provided, state whether the paraphrase is acceptable or unacceptable. If it is unacceptable, explain why. Then, offer a better paraphrase and explain why yours is better.

Rob

Focused Topic: How the development of the railroads increased the movement west and changed the nature of those who went.

Thesis: Without the construction of the Transcontinental Railroad in 1869, the United States of America could quite possibly have developed east-west differences even more significant than those that divided the northern and southern states.

Original Text of Rob's Source:

> The eastern United States had become markedly English with a strong French influence. Urbanites and those who lived in small towns witnessed the evolution of an aristocracy, especially among the cash-wealthy merchants and service professionals, whose houses and gardens began to imitate the manor homes of the British and French aristocracy. Lace, satin, velvet, polished wood and vast quantities of glass proclaimed the status of the persons whose homes they adorned. Paved streets were straight and lined with trees, and the community met and mingled on front porches and verandahs where news was spread and gossip shared. From the coldest sea-coast village of Maine to the hottest and most humid Georgia plantation, the aspirations for "the good life" and the accoutrements of that life were more similar than different.

Rob's paraphrase:

> The east had become very English and French. Those who lived in cities and small towns saw the development of an upper class among wealthy merchants, whose houses and yards looked like the manor homes of the aristocracy of England and France. Materials like lace, satin, velvet, wood, glass announced the wealth of the people who lived in the houses decorated like that. Streets were paved and straight, and tree-lined. Front porches and verandahs were where the community gathered and where news and gossip were shared. From Maine to Georgia plantation, what people considered "the good life" was very similar.

Is Rob's paraphrase acceptable?

Why or why not?

If Rob's paraphrase is unacceptable, provide an example of what would make it better:

Why is your paraphrase better?

EXERCISE FOUR:

PRACTICING PARAPHRASE

Now, apply to your own research paper what you've learned and practiced. Select a key passage from one of your more important sources and paraphrase it. Then, share the original passage and your paraphrase with a partner and have him/her answer the following questions:

Is this paraphrase acceptable?

Why or why not?

What could be done to make this paraphrase better?

18. How do I keep my research organized?

While you examine your sources and take notes, you will want to keep three things always before you: the final statement of your focused topic, your preliminary thesis, and your preliminary outline.

As you take notes, whatever form those notes take—whether you handwrite them on 3 x 5 index cards (as was the accepted method until the proliferation of the personal computer) or type your notes on your computer; whether you quote, paraphrase, or summarize—*each individual note* should be accompanied by an identification of the source of that information and the notation of where that information fits in your preliminary outline.

Here's a sample of Ella's notes:

from: Berkline, Jarvis. "A handful of adventurers." <u>History Alive</u>.
November 2006: 87-115.*

II. A.

First landing consisted of 104 "men and boys." (QT)

39 were members of the ships' crews.

1 died in the Caribbean. (88)

The Roman numeral and capital letter at the top of the note indicate the location in the outline. The QT beside the material in quotation marks reminds Ella that this phrase is quoted directly from the source. The number in parentheses indicates the page number of the printed source.

from: Berkline, Jarvis. "A handful of adventurers." <u>*History Alive.*</u>
November 2006: 87-115.*

III. B. 3. —(SUM/PPHRASE)

Jamestown Island (which is really a peninsula) is swampy. (100)

Being isolated as an island or a peninsula connected to the mainland by only a narrow isthmus, it was inhabited by very little large game like deer and bears. (101)

The settlers quickly killed off all the game of their tiny area and had to search for more suitable hunting locations. (101)

from: Jamestown Historical Society Web Site. Aug. 2006. 31 May 2008.
<http://jameshistsoc.org>.

II. B.

"<u>*eight Dutchmen*</u> *[probably German farmers] and Poles [craftsmen hired by the Virginia Company to help establish the colony's manufacturing capabilities]" (QT).*

Notice that, at this point, Ella's notes are not coming in the order of her outline. That's because the author of each individual source is following his or her *own* outline. Ella will be able to organize her information according to her preliminary outline before she writes her first draft, based on *her* outline designations.

*from: Jamestown Historical Society Web Site. Aug. 2006. 31 May 2008.
<http://jameshistsoc.org>.*

III. D.—(SUM/PPHRASE)

expressed strong frustration with the colony and colonists. They demanded in writing that the colonists send goods (furs, precious metals, etc.) with enough value to repay the cost of initial voyage. Also, a lump of gold to prove that they had found the South Sea, and one member of the lost Roanoke Colony.

You've probably noticed that, so far, Ella's notes are only bits of information directly from her sources; she has indicated no reactions to her sources or original ideas. As she generates these responses and ideas, she will take them down *just like notes directly from her sources*, and she will mark them in the same way. The only difference will be that she will not have a source to cite.

from Jamestown: Fragile Seeds

I.—(ME)

My question: >>Is it any wonder we evolved into such a materialistic society since, at our very roots, the United States was little more than an investment, a speculative venture?<<

Remember that Ella devised the double-caret mark and the code at the beginning and end of the note, and she introduced the note with the code, "ME" (see pages 140–142) as a visual means of identifying those notes that were her own thoughts. She has also stated that these notes are her questions and observations.

from: Jamestown: Fragile Seeds

V.—(ME)

It seems to me: >> future colonies probably fared better from the beginning because they learned (1) to send the right people (people who had a real desire to begin a new life and who were willing to work to build that life), (2) for the right reason (people who are asking to leave, not being bribed or threatened). <<

If this is your first major research project, keeping track of every source for every note and keying every note to your preliminary outline might seem tedious and time-consuming, but being diligent now will help you be extremely well prepared when you need to be.

Here are some of the pitfalls that keeping track of your sources and outline will help you prevent:

> You'll cover your entire outline and not turn in an incomplete, unbalanced paper. *As you take notes*, if you find holes in your outline, you know well in advance that you must look specifically for that information.

> You won't get lost following an interesting, but irrelevant, tangent. You probably already know how seductive the Internet can be, when all you have to do is click on a link and then another and another to follow a fascinating thread from site to site. Before long, however, you find you've lost sight of what you were originally looking up. Therefore, no matter how interesting a line of inquiry might be, if it's not something you set out to look up (as indicated in your preliminary outline), ignore it. *If you can't put an outline notation with the note, do not take the note!*

> You won't end up accidentally committing plagiarism by failing to properly cite a source. At some point in your academic career, such an "error" could result in a failing grade for the project *or the entire course*; disciplinary action—including the possibility of being expelled from the school or denied your degree; or even professional disciplinary action (being disbarred as a lawyer or losing your medical credentials, etc.). Later, we'll talk more about the penalties for even accidental plagiarism and how to avoid them.

EXERCISE FIVE:

EXAMINING AND CRITIQUING RESEARCH NOTES

Here are a few samples of Rob's notes. Examine them and then answer the questions that follow to help him as he continues his research.

Rob

Focused Topic*:* How the development of the railroads increased the movement west and changed the nature of those who went.

Preliminary Thesis*:* Without the construction of the Transcontinental Railroad in 1869, the United States of America could quite possibly have developed east-west differences even more significant than those that divided the northern and southern states.

From: *The Growth of a Nation* (DVD)

The Transcon RR was first dreamed of as a means to unify northern states during the Civil War.

//I wonder how the War would have gone if the RR had been built earlier?//

Kansas–Nebraska Act of 1854 was supposed to clear the way for Transcon RR.

Popular sovereignty: Congress would not decide whether territory would have slaves but people in territory would.

Lincoln–Douglas Debates

...virtually nullified the Missouri Compromise of 1820 and the Compromise of 1850.

California admitted as a free state in 1850.

Texas was a slave state.

Because of its distance from the front lines, Texas was a "supply state" for the Confederacy, contributing soldiers, especially cavalry. Texans fought in every major battle of the War.

Texas was separated from the rest of the Confederacy when the North captured the Mississippi, making large movements of men or supplies impossible.

The last battle of the Civil War was fought in Texas.

Slavery not prohibited in territory of New Mexico.

What are some strengths of Rob's notes so far?

What are some weaknesses of Rob's notes so far?

EXERCISE SIX:

REVIEWING YOUR OWN RESEARCH NOTES

Now, apply to your own research paper what you've learned and practiced. Review the notes you've taken so far. Make certain that you've noted the source of *each* note and identified where the information in that note fits in your preliminary outline. Also, remember to clearly identify quotes and paraphrases with an abbreviation or some sort of symbol.

19. How do I protect myself from charges of plagiarism?—1

The answer to this question is simply do not submit someone else's work and call it yours. Don't even imply that someone else's work is yours.

Remember that plagiarism ranges from using information from a source without giving that source appropriate credit to turning in someone else's paper as your own work.

The most obvious cases of plagiarism—and there have been several fairly high-profile cases lately, from an Ivy League-university student's incorporating lengthy passages from her favorite author in her own "debut" novel, to a *Harry Potter* fan's publishing a compendium of Potter trivia, *none of which he created*—involve directly taking someone else's words and ideas and using them in a different context. If you do not have the permission of the person who originally created the words and ideas and if you do not give credit to that person, you are committing plagiarism.

You should know that there are many software applications available that help teachers scan student work, diagnose possible occurrences of plagiarism, and even identify the source(s) of the plagiarized material. If you cheat, then, there is a *very strong* chance that you will be caught, and the consequences can be disastrous.

The avoidance of plagiarism, then, begins at the note-taking stage, the stage at which you are (rightfully) gathering information from a number of sources for the express purpose of presenting that information in your paper.

Here's how to help prevent *even the appearance of plagiarism* while still in the note taking stages:

1. Keep an extremely detailed and complete record of where you got each piece of information.

We've already discussed this in sections 17 and 18, but it highlights the importance of being organized and keeping track of your sources.

2. Find and use multiple sources for the same information.

In Chapter Three, part of your evaluation of potential sources included whether the factual information could be verified from other sources. A good research paper will never rely on a single source for any— especially key—information. Having *at least two sources* for each fact, or at least two expert views on each issue, will help prevent your creating the impression that you are the originator of any of that information.

3. Take real notes; do not merely cut and paste.

Remember that, ultimately, you are supposed to be learning something about your subject, not just moving around blocks of information. Therefore, whether you are handwriting your notes or keyboarding them, go through the process of creating your own notes. Even if you are copying material you do intend to quote, copy or retype it. Do not merely take a block of text from the source and paste it into a word processing document. The more you cut and paste (even if you intend to "change" the material later), the more you increase the chances that words and ideas that are not yours will find their way into your final paper.

In section 17, we talked about notes that were direct quotations from your source, notes that were direct paraphrases or summaries of a source, and notes that reflected your own ideas. This is one of the reasons for taking three different kinds of notes and being aware *every step of the way* what kind of note you are taking.

EXERCISE SEVEN:

EVALUATING STUDENT WORK FOR POTENTIAL PLAGIARISM

What follows are excerpts from sources Rob is using for his research paper on the Transcontinental Railroad. Following each are two drafts of the parts of his paper in which he is planning to use that information. Beside each draft, state whether you think Rob is vulnerable to a charge of plagiarism and explain why or why not. If you feel he is in danger of being accused of plagiarism, what can he do to fix it?

1. **Here's the original text, from Rob's United States history textbook:**

> The first Transcontinental Railroad in the United States, largely motivated by a desire to bind the Union together during the Civil War, was officially completed in the historic "golden spike" ceremony at Promontory Summit, Utah, on May 10, 1869. This railroad, that linked the already-thriving eastern railway network with California and the Pacific Ocean, would forever alter the population and economy of the West. The wagon trains of previous decades became obsolete overnight, and many say that the West was opened to a new breed of softer, greedier pioneer. This new, modern transportation system substantially increased the migration of white homesteaders and exacerbated the decline of Native Americans in these regions

Here's the first draft of this section of his paper:

> The first Transcontinental Railroad in the United States, was largely motivated by a desire to join the Union together during the Civil War. However, it was not officially completed until 1869. This railroad linked the eastern railway network, which was already thriving, with California and the Pacific Ocean. It would forever alter the population and economy of the West. Wagon trains became obsolete. The West was opened to a new breed of pioneer. This railroad greatly increased the migration of white homesteaders and sped up the decline of Native Americans in these regions. (Smith 223)

Is Rob risking a charge of plagiarism?

Why or why not?

If he is, what can he do to correct his problem?

Here's the second draft:

> Jonas Smith, in his Pulitzer-Prize-winning chronicle of the building of the railroad, suggests the irony that the project was originally conceived as a means to facilitate the transport of Union soldiers and supplies during the Civil War, but it was not finished until four years after the war was over (222). With the completion of the railroad, however, Smith notes, "The wagon trains of previous decades became obsolete overnight, and many say that the West was opened to a new breed of softer, greedier pioneer" (223). The ease with which the trip from the civilized East to the wild West could be made "increased the migration of white homesteaders and exacerbated the decline of Native Americans in these regions" (223).

Is Rob risking a charge of plagiarism?

Why or why not?

If he is, what can he do to correct his problem?

2. Here's the original text, from one of Rob's printed sources:

> While it did not span the continent from the Atlantic coast to the Pacific, the technologically miraculous rail line that crossed the Great Plains and the Rocky Mountains, linking Omaha, Nebraska, with Sacramento, California, in the 1860s is exalted with the title, "First Transcontinental Railroad." Yet, while this famous line traverses barely half of the nation's girth, when linked with the already-thriving Eastern network of railroads, the line did, in fact, complete a nationwide network of relatively comfortable and fast transportation that would render the wagon train and stagecoach obsolete and transform the population of the American West.

Here's the first draft of this section of his paper:

> The First Transcontinental Railroad is not given that name because it actually spanned the continent from the Atlantic coast to the Pacific, but because completion of the Omaha-to-Sacramento line was linked with a network of Eastern railroads that already existed. It completed a train system in which a passenger could board a train in any eastern city and step off the train in California. The relative comfort and speed offered by the railroad quickly made the slow and uncomfortable stagecoach obsolete. The wagon train, too.

Is Rob risking a charge of plagiarism?

Why or why not?

If he is, what can he do to correct his problem?

Here's the second draft:

> Virtually every historian acknowledges that the First Transcontinental Railroad is not given that name because it actually spanned the continent from the Atlantic coast to the Pacific, but because completion of the Omaha-to-Sacramento line was linked with a network of Eastern railroads that already existed. It completed a train system in which a passenger could board a train in any Eastern city and step off the train in California. The relative comfort and speed offered by the railroad quickly made the slow and uncomfortable stagecoach obsolete. The wagon train, too.

Is Rob risking a charge of plagiarism?

Why or why not?

If he is, what can he do to correct his problem?

3. Here's the original text, from one of Rob's Internet sources:

Odd Facts and Interesting Trivia About the TCR:

> The famous "Golden Spike" ceremony, which was to mark the completion of the railroad, took place on May 10, 1869.

> In 1879, the United States Supreme Court formally established the "official" date of completion of the Transcontinental Railroad as November 6, 1869.

> At its completion, the TCR was not directly connected to the Eastern U.S. rail network. Instead, trains had to be ferried across the Missouri River. In 1872, the Union Pacific Missouri River Bridge, which finally connected the East and West, opened.

> The Central Pacific (building the railroad from west to east) laid 690 miles (1,110 km) of track, starting in Sacramento, California, and continuing through California and Nevada, joining the Union Pacific line at Promontory Summit in the Utah Territory.

> The Union Pacific (working from east to west) laid 1,087 miles (1,749 km) of track, starting in Council Bluffs, Iowa, and continuing across the Missouri River and through Nebraska, the Colorado Territory, the Wyoming Territory, and the Utah Territory, joining the Central Pacific at Promontory Summit.

> Modern-day Interstate 80 closely follows the path of the TCR, with one exception. Between Echo, Utah, and Wells, Nevada, Interstate 80 passes through Salt Lake City along the south shore of the Great Salt Lake. The Railroad followed the Weber River to Ogden coinciding with the route of Interstate 84, around the north side of the Great Salt Lake.

Here's the first draft of this section of his paper:

> *The Official Website of the First Transcontinental Railroad notes in its "Odd Facts and Interesting Trivia" section that, at its completion, the TCR was not directly connected to the Eastern U.S. rail network. Instead, trains had to be ferried across the Missouri River. In 1872, the Union Pacific Missouri River Bridge, which connected the East and West, opened. They also say that modern-day Interstate 80 closely follows the path of the TCR, with one exception. Between Echo, Utah, and Wells, Nevada, Interstate 80 passes through Salt Lake City along the south shore of the Great Salt Lake. The Railroad followed the Weber River to Ogden coinciding with the route of Interstate 84, north of the Lake.*

Is Rob risking a charge of plagiarism?

Why or why not?

If he is, what can he do to correct his problem?

Here's the second draft:

> *The Official Website of the First Transcontinental Railroad notes in its "Odd Facts and Interesting Trivia" section that, "at its completion, the TCR was not directly connected to the Eastern U.S. rail network. Instead, trains had to be ferried across the Missouri River. In 1872, the Union Pacific Missouri River Bridge, which connected the East and West, opened." They also say that "modern-day Interstate 80 closely follows the path of the TCR, with one exception. Between Echo, Utah, and Wells, Nevada, Interstate 80 passes through Salt Lake City along the south shore of the Great Salt Lake. The Railroad followed the Weber River to Ogden coinciding with the route of Interstate 84, north of the Lake."*

Is Rob risking a charge of plagiarism?

Why or why not?

If he is, what can he do to correct his problem?

20. How do I begin refining my thesis and outline?

It would be very naïve to think that, after more than a month of research, you'll submit a final draft that argues the precise thesis you started out with. While your thesis guided your search for sources and your note taking, if you really allowed yourself to learn from your sources, you have surely encountered facts you did not expect and experts whose interpretations of facts were not exactly what you'd anticipated.

For example, **Ella's** preliminary thesis was: *Changes in the management of the Jamestown settlement helped define the nature of future British colonies in North America—and eventually the United States.*

She has learned that the Jamestown settlement was originally a business venture financed by the Virginia Company and that the challenges faced by the settlers and the company's ultimate financial failure resulted in the colony's reverting to the Crown. She's found much more information, however, on the initial challenges faced by the settlers, the reasons for some of those challenges, and how they were overcome. *These factors*, she has decided, had a greater impact on how future colonies were founded and managed than the actual changes in Jamestown's management.

Therefore, she adjusts her thesis to read: *The near-failure of the Jamestown settlement taught important lessons about how and why colonies should be established in North America and helped define the nature of future colonial ventures.*

Ella probably does not need to consult her teacher about this revision to her thesis because, while it does reflect where her sources are leading her, it does not fundamentally change the project she set out to accomplish. She will still be writing about the settlement of Jamestown and its impact on future American colonies. Anything requiring a deeper change—from a focus on Jamestown to one on the Plymouth Plantation, for example, would probably necessitate Ella's getting her instructor's okay. Such a change requires a new preliminary outline and probably an extension to her deadline—something the instructor might not be able to approve.

It is, therefore, very important to think carefully about your topic from the very beginning. It is expected that your thesis will be revised at least once. It is *not* expected that you will change your focus completely.

EXERCISE EIGHT:

EXAMINING REVISED THESES

Look at Rob's proposed revision and see whether or not it is warranted and advisable.

Rob

Focused Topic*:* How the development of the railroads increased the movement west and changed the nature of those who went.

Preliminary Thesis*:* Without the construction of the Transcontinental Railroad in 1869, the United States of America could quite possibly have developed east-west differences even more significant than those that divided the northern and southern states.

Revised Thesis*: The Transcontinental Railroad, completed in 1869, opened the floodgates for white migration to the West and made possible the United States as we know it today.*

Rob's Reasons for Revision*: "It seems clearer and easier to understand. All of my sources talk about the rush of settlers to the West and how the Native American population declined."*

Is Rob's proposed revision acceptable?

Why or why not?

Are the reasons for Rob's proposed revision acceptable?

Why or why not?

EXERCISE NINE:

EXAMINING YOUR THESIS FOR POTENTIAL REVISION

Now, apply to your own research project what you've learned and practiced. Examine your topic and thesis and experiment with any revisions to your thesis that you think might make your paper stronger.

Chapter
5

SEEING THE FOREST AND THE TREES

21. How do I know when I've done enough research?

Many professional writers never feel they've done enough research, that there's always something more to learn, one more source to explore…

The reality of the situation, however, is that you have a paper to write and turn in, and the due date is, indeed, more than merely a guideline. There are, however, a few very practical ways to determine when you're "done" with the research and ready to begin drafting the paper.

First of all, look at your preliminary outline and your notes. If you're approaching the end of your research, you should have several notes for each section of your preliminary outline, and there should be some balance among the sections. *If you find you have no notes for one or more sections of your outline, or some sections contain far fewer notes than others, you're not yet done.*

Second, review your notes. You know you've done a really thorough job researching and are finished when you have the same—or very similar—information from several sources. Chances are, you already have enough information if you're not finding anything new as you look at additional sources. You also know you're essentially done when your sources start to refer to each other. If Jones begins to cite Smith as a source, and you've already taken notes from Smith, you're ready to write your paper.

Finally, check your research schedule. How much time do you have left before the paper is due? Does your teacher intend to collect first drafts and provide feedback before you write the final draft? You must make certain you finish your research and leave enough time to do an excellent job on these final stages. After all, why throw away all your hard work of the past several weeks by dashing off a second- or third-rate paper because you didn't leave yourself enough time?

22. How do I get ready to write?

Actually, you're the best one to answer that question. Short of procrastinating until it's too late or buying your paper from an online "paper mill" (and there is a *very strong chance* you will be caught if you do that), how you organize your sources, adjust your seat, set the preferences on your computer are all matters of personal choice. Still, there are a few things you can do to facilitate the writing process and to smooth the transition from researching to writing:

1. **Put everything away.** You might not want to return books, magazines, and disks (CD, DVD, etc.) to the library yet—you may need to verify a fact, a spelling, or a page number—but things you've taken from your own shelves can be reshelved. Scraps of paper, pages you printed or photocopied can be gathered up and filed safely. Give yourself a clean, clutter-free, and distraction-free place to work.

2. **Gather your tools.** What's your process? Do you handwrite everything first and then type it onto your computer when it's done? If so, get your pencils, pens, pads (or notebook) together. Do you compose at the keyboard? Make sure everything is working and ready. Be sure you have enough ink and paper in the printer. You do not want to be plagued by interruptions once you sit down and actually begin writing your paper.

3. **Organize your formal list of sources.** Very shortly, you will have to have to begin formally referring to your sources, citing page numbers, quoting, providing attributions, all of those nuts-and-bolts things that help differentiate a research paper from a mere essay. Now is a good time to create the list of attributions and documentation that will eventually become your Works Cited Page. (You'll find an overview of the appropriate formats specified by the Modern Languages Association, MLA, on page 196.) Doing this now will also help you make sure you're accounting for and crediting every source—another means of avoiding the devastating charge of plagiarism.

4. **Organize and review your notes.** This is the last step before actually beginning to write your paper. As you took your notes, beside each one you indicated where it fit in your preliminary outline. At this point, all that information (possibly hundreds of individual notes) is in no particular order. Now is the time to sequence them according to their Roman numeral, capital letter, Arabic numeral, etc.

Once you have your notes in order, read through them. Remember, depending on how long you've been working on this paper, some of your notes might be several weeks old. You might not remember all of the information you've collected. You might not remember some of the questions you were asking yourself or some of the objections you intended to raise. You might not be aware of some contradictions between your sources or of some excessive repetition. You'll want to refresh yourself on all of these concerns. Most importantly, however, you want to make certain your topic and how you're going to discuss it are fresh in your mind.

5. **Freewrite your introduction.** This is really a part of the composing process, so it technically does not belong in this section, but many successful writers find it very helpful to write the introductions to their longer papers at least a full day before the rest of the paper. This "introduction" is really more of a broad overview, but writing it gives you one last chance to review your information and begin to frame *in your mind* the words you are going to use to present it.

Make certain your thesis is clearly stated somewhere in this introduction.

Now, stop procrastinating and begin writing.

23. How do I protect myself from charges of plagiarism?—2

Please understand that charges of plagiarism can have devastating consequences in college, graduate school, and professional life. Students have been placed on "academic probation," have been expelled from school, and have lost memberships in student and professional societies as a result of charges of plagiarism. Professional writers have been fined and have actually lost their jobs as the result of charges of plagiarism.

Your best defense, therefore, is to know how to present information from outside sources, how to quote appropriately, and how to document the information and sources you use.

To present someone else's words as if they were your words, or to present information you got from someone else without giving that person credit is

> unfair (We all want to be acknowledged for our work and our contribution to a project.)

> unethical (Professionals especially rely on receiving credit for their work because it is on the basis of that credit that they receive promotions, pay raises, and other opportunities to advance professionally. Non-professionals also rely on receiving credit for their work to qualify them for advanced study or to open professional opportunities for them.)

> illegal (The written ideas of others; their song lyrics; musical notations; painted, sculpted, photographed, or filmed artwork; their poetry, short stories, novels, plays, informative articles; etc., are all included in the definition of "intellectual property." Intellectual property is just as real as physical property, and it is protected by law. That's what a copyright is: the declaration that the holder of the copyright "owns" the right to make copies of the work, or to give permission to someone else to make copies. To violate a copyright is to steal someone else's property and is punishable by law: expulsion from school, lawsuit, fine, etc.).

Many people in the academic world consider plagiarism—the use of someone else's ideas or words without permission and without proper documentation—to be the worst crime that can be committed in academia.

There are, however, several things you can do in the writing stage of your project to avoid accidentally committing plagiarism and to avoid being unfairly accused of plagiarism.

1. Begin every quotation with its attribution (and do not present any quotation without one).

Here's how **Ella** has been handling quotations in the first draft of her paper:

> Frances Abnigail, in her groundbreaking study of the impact of race on the first English settlement, suggests, "The early British, having been relatively isolated from racial diversity, had not yet been tainted by the ..."
>
> Abnigail continues to insist, "To try to separate the settlers' fear from their prejudice is to grossly oversimplify..."

2. Be transparent. Discuss the sources as you discuss the material you got from the sources. If you remember what we suggested as one of the purposes of the research paper—to learn something independently and then to report on what you learned and how you learned it—you won't have trouble. Look at excerpts from **Ella's** draft:

> While Gallant's overview is clearly a simplified account for children, he still raises some important points that earlier historians merely gloss over, including the fact that the Jamestown colony was intended to be, first and foremost, a moneymaking venture...
>
> Goddard's emphasis is the same, with a brilliant explanation of exactly how the colony was supposed to make its investors rich: "...
>
> The pseudo-academic Americans for Truth, Justice, and the American Way, however, take a more idealistic approach. Their website seems to insist that all settlers in the colony were trustworthy, loyal, and brave...
>
> Both Goddard and Abnigail would disagree, insisting that...

3. Have something to add to the conversation; don't merely report on what your sources said. Throughout your note taking, in addition to direct quotation and paraphrase/summary, you've been taking notes that reflect your ideas: questions that occurred to you; contradictions you noted; evaluation, analysis, and interpretation of your sources; even original ideas. These all become the basis of your paper. The material you gathered from your sources is there merely to support your ideas.

Again, here are a few examples from **Ella's** draft:

> Captain Smith, in a letter to his son, justified his treatment of the natives as, "altogethre necessarye for the survivyal of mine countryemen and the sucesse of thysse endeavour" (Virtual Jamestown). Still, given their certain knowledge of the fates of the Ajacàn Mission and the Roanoke Colony, one must wonder what the settlers were expecting. It certainly seems as if any European travelers to the New World would have presumed hostility from the people whose land they were invading, rather than expressing surprise at their often unfriendly greeting...
>
> Still, there is every reason to believe that John Rolfe truly loved his wife Pocahontas and mourned her after her death. Certainly the statue he erected in her honor in London would indicate that...

Allowing your paper to become something of a dialogue between you and your sources (and a conversation among your sources as well) rather than merely a massive dump of information, is probably the most effective way to avoid charges of plagiarism—and write a dynamite paper in the process.

EXERCISE ONE:

CHECKING FOR POTENTIAL PLAGIARISM

Let's look at an excerpt from Rob's paper to see whether he is vulnerable to charges of plagiarism, and how he might fix it if he is.

Rob

"The idea of securing Chinese labor arose because they had already helped build the California Central Railroad that ran from Sacramento to Marysville. The Chinese had also built the San Jose Railway. Critics of the idea originally thought the diminutive Chinese were too small to tackle such a momentous task. Charles Crocker of Central Pacific pointed out, however, that 'the Chinese made the Great Wall, didn't they?'"

"The first Chinese were hired in 1865 for approximately $28 per month. Their assignment was to do the very dangerous work of blasting, and laying ties over the treacherous terrain of the high Sierras. These noble and hardworking 'foreigners' lived in simple huts and cooked their own meals of fish, dried oysters and fruit, mushrooms and seaweed."

"The work was difficult and progressed slowly; the terrain on which they were laying track rose 7,000 feet in 100 miles. To conquer the many nearly perpendicular slopes, workers used techniques they had learned in China. They were lowered in baskets by ropes from the top of cliffs in baskets. While hanging there, they chipped away at the granite and planted explosives."

Is Rob in danger of being accused of committing plagiarism?

Why or why not?

Choose one or two of his paragraphs and fix them for him (create fictitious sources if you choose. The exercise here is how to handle them in the text of the paper). As your model, follow the excerpts from Ella's papers we showed you on pages 177–178.)

EXERCISE TWO:

EXAMINING YOUR OWN WORK FOR POTENTIAL PLAGIARISM

Now, apply to your own research project what you've learned and practiced. Share a page or so of what you have written so far with a partner. Have him or her read your excerpt and answer the following questions, while you read his or her excerpt and answer them as well.

Is your partner in danger of being accused of committing plagiarism?

Why or why not?

Choose one or two paragraphs from your partner's excerpt and fix them.

Chapter
6

WRITING YOUR RESEARCH PAPER

24. What am I aiming for?

Let's return for just a second to our original definition of a research paper from Chapter 1:

> A research paper is a thesis-driven essay that uses relevant, credible sources to support its ideas and arguments.

What this means, then, is that what you are writing is essentially an essay, and it must be structured like an essay with an **introduction**, a **body**, and a **conclusion**.

It is, however, a specific type of essay—*a thesis-driven* essay. Therefore, your introduction must introduce your thesis and then present a broad overview of the information you will present to support that thesis.

Our definition also specifies that this essay uses *sources to support...ideas and arguments.* Therefore, the **body** of this essay will look like what we've been examining and practicing above: a presentation of your information, citation and attribution of your sources, analysis and evaluation of your sources, along with your own insights and reflection.

Finally, because your research paper has been defined as a close-cousin to a persuasive paper (*thesis-driven, support, arguments*), your **conclusion** must sum up the evidence presented and establish the validity of your point—your thesis.

As you write, you will keep your outline and your notes close at hand. Your outline informed your notetaking (and each note should be coded with the outline notation for where you intend to use that information in your paper). Writing this draft is not a matter of deciding what to say where— those decisions have already been made. Your task at hand is *simply* to flesh everything out—just as you've practiced in the previous exercises.

All along, since we have been presuming all that Ella, Rob, and you are all working on a 6-10 page paper (and you should always try to fulfill the maximum guideline if you want that A+), you should assume you need a 1-2 page introduction, a 6-7 page body (remember, just discussing your sources and transitioning from one point to another will require some space), and a 1-page conclusion.

25. How should I use my sources in my paper?

We've already paid a good deal of attention to how you discuss, quote from, analyze, and evaluate your sources in your paper. The key point to remember is simply that this is a research paper and not merely a report. Your research paper is to be *thesis-driven* (not source-driven). It is supposed to use information from sources to *support* its arguments and ideas. You, therefore, need to present only information that *applies directly to your thesis*, and you will use as many words discussing, analyzing, and evaluating your sources *and sharing your own conclusions and insights* as you use quoting, paraphrasing, and summarizing your sources.

> ...you will use as many words discussing, analyzing, and evaluating your sources *and sharing your own conclusions and insights* as you use quoting, paraphrasing, and summarizing your sources.

Here are a few additional guidelines about using your sources in a top-grade research paper:

> quote *only* when the words you are quoting are so specific or technical that you *absolutely cannot* paraphrase or summarize without losing some of the impact of the original wording;

> keep quotations short, certainly not more than a full paragraph—and even that long should be rare;

> *never* string two or more quotations together without some discussion of your own in between;

> given the nature of an introduction and conclusion, yours should not contain material that needs to be cited and attributed;

> overall, if more than 2/3 of your paper seems to be coming from your sources and less than 1/3 from you, you are very close to writing a report and not a research paper;

> finally, if you find yourself not attributing a source or two on every page (except your introduction and conclusion), you are either writing an essay or committing plagiarism.

Basically, if you remember that the thesis at the center of your paper is *your thesis*, and the material from your sources exists only to support your thesis, you'll be all right. If you remember that the core of your paper is *your* insight, and that the source material exists only to support that insight and to help explain how you arrived at that insight, you'll be fine.

EXERCISE ONE:

CRITIQUING FIRST DRAFTS

Here are a few excerpts from Rob's first draft. They demonstrate some things he has done fairly well and some things that will need to be improved in revision. Read the excerpts and then provide a brief critique of each.

Rob

> The first Chinese were hired in 1865 for approximately $28 per month. Their assignment was to do the very dangerous work of blasting, and laying ties over the treacherous terrain of the high Sierras. While Pendleton uses this figure as support for his charge of racism, because the Chinese were paid so little for such difficult work, Marshall points out that the going rate for railroad work was only $20 a month, and some workers were paid even less than that.

What has Rob done right in this excerpt?

What does Rob need to improve when he revises?

26. How do I continue to protect myself from charges of plagiarism?

At this point, you'd almost have to be committing intentional plagiarism in order to be accused of it. Discuss your topic in your own words. When you present information you took from a source, give that source credit. Do not over quote. Attribute the quotation to its source before the quotation. Don't panic or get too self-assured, and you'll be fine.

27. How much time will I need to write my paper?

In Chapter 2, we claimed that, with all of the preliminary materials in place, you could possibly write the first draft of your paper in a few hours. *This is true because this is the stage where you put into words the ideas you have already thought of and noted.*

Only you, however, know how fast those words are likely to come to you. Some people are very fast writers, and it might take them an evening to write 10 pages of material.

Remember, now is *not* the stage when you are generating new ideas—that step is done.

Other people are slower writers and find themselves staring at their computer screen (or blank sheet of paper) for long periods waiting for the *right words* to come.

Which are you? Be honest with yourself, and pace yourself accordingly. Remember that you'll want to put at least one day between "finishing" this first draft and reading it again with an eye toward revision.

28. What does a good first draft look like?

We're calling this a "first draft" and not a "rough draft" for one very good reason. If you take the word "rough" too literally, your draft might end up needing so much revision that you'd still be several drafts—and several weeks—away from something you'd actually want to turn in for a grade.

For our purposes (and the purposes of the highest grade possible on your final draft), you should set out to make this draft as good as it can possibly be. In a perfect world, you'd write a draft so good it wouldn't need any revision.

Of course, such a world doesn't exist, but that is what you should aim for in this first draft stage.

Here is Ella's first draft. Notice how she has tried to make it read like her paper. She has even included her documentation.

The Lessons of Jamestown

by Ella

With Christopher Columbus's discovery of what the Europeans called the "New World," a mad scramble began to colonize the land and exploit the vast natural resources of this New World. Spain, the nation that had funded Columbus's voyages and was, without a doubt, the most powerful nation in the world at the time, had already established several successful colonies, as had France, another world power. England, however, desiring very strongly to take its place as a world power beside its two neighbors—and enemies—had not yet succeeded. Sir Walter Raleigh's Roanoke had failed, and Elizabeth died without having established her foothold in North America.

James I, however, refused to watch his rivals build empires while he was stuck in England. He longed for an American colony, and eventually, his desire was fulfilled by the Jamestown Plantation, a commercial venture of the Virginia Company. This poorly-planned and badly-staffed venture nearly failed a number

---

of times. The colony's near failure and the lessons learned in **[Here is Ella's thesis**.] overcoming them helped shape the nature of future British settlements in America and the nature of the future United States itself.

What the British learned from the near-failure that was **[We are still in Ella's introduction. Here is where she mentions the specific points she is going to discuss in detail and with support in the body of her paper**.] Jamestown was that, in order for a settlement to succeed, the settlers had to have a vested interest in settling. People fleeing some sort of persecution or freeing themselves from debt or just seeking a new start would fight for the success of their settlement more fiercely than mere employees or servants would. They also learned that, if they were going to build a new life in a new land, they would need *all* of the requirements of a life—including the companionship of women. They also learned important lessons about relations with the aboriginal natives and they learned something about the demands of the land. They also learned what people needed to be included in the first wave of settlers to a new colony.

The branch of the Virginia Company that established Jamestown was called The London Company (Goddard 73). A rival branch, the Plymouth Company, was established at the same time, but never fulfilled its charter (Goddard 73). The first Jamestown settlers sailed in three ships, leaving England in December 1606. James I assigned them three goals: **[This paragraph coincides with Roman Numeral I of Ella's preliminary outline.]** find gold, find a viable trade route to Asia, and find the Lost Colony of Roanoke. ("Colonial Library" 275). Already the mission was challenged, not only **[Ella certainly does not waste a lot of time on background of the colonial movement or the formation of the Virginia Company. She gets right into the issue of reasons for the settlement's failure.]** because of the bad weather that delayed the voyage, but because none of the reasons for the settlement was of importance to more than a few of the settlers. Most were, essentially, little more than underpaid employees of the Virginia Company. The investors, who had the most to gain from the venture's success, stayed safely in London. [*So far, Ella has tended to over-document. The fact that there is no documentation here suggests that Ella is sharing some of her ideas or insight with us.*] By the same token, the settlers—even the ones who expected to make their own fortune, as well as the fortunes of their investors—probably cared very little about James's desire for an empire and for a full royal treasury. Had more of the settlers themselves had more of a personal interest in the success of their settlement, they might have worked, if not harder, certainly smarter.

Rolls of the original 105 settlers show that the passengers of those first three ships included six members of the Council, one [*Now, we are in Roman Numeral II of Ella's preliminary outline.*] member of the clergy, 49 "gentlemen," 13 laborers (including 1 surgeon), and four boys (Virtual Jamestown). The rest were craftsmen: a tailor, a bricklayer, a barber, etc. (Virtual Jamestown). What each man's—there were no women on this first voyage—reason for wanting to come to America may have been is not known. Some were probably seeking adventure. Some were probably hoping to start a new life. But for all of them, their personal reasons for the venture were largely overlooked, certainly not recorded by history, in favor of the commercial goals of finding gold and a trade route to Asia.

This first band of settlers was also poorly suited for carving a new civilization out of a strange and uninhabitable wilderness. In May 1607, when they finally reached land, in the territory they were calling Virginia, they chose an island about 40 miles inland from where the Atlantic Ocean ends and the Chesapeake Bay begins. They called the river the James River (after King James) and chose the spot because they thought the land would be easy to defend if they were attacked by sea by a European power like France or Spain ("Jamestown Fort Discovered" C-27). They also thought the [*These paragraphs coincide with Roman Numeral III of Ella's preliminary outline.*] plentiful water would make farming easier ("Jamestown Fort Discovered" C-27).

But they were mistaken. They quickly learned that the land they chose was marshy. They were plagued by swarms of mosquitoes. The river where they chose to settle was still salty water and highly influenced by the ocean's tides. The surrounding area was also inhabited by Indians ("Jamestown Fort Discovered" C-27). They attacked almost immediately and proved to be on-again-off-again enemies to the settlers throughout Jamestown's existence. Marshy land led to crop failures. The island's isolation meant that it lacked the large game animals that would be needed to feed the entire population. The "gentlemen," of course, refused to work, as such was beneath their station, so the tasks of building a fort, storehouse, church, and dwellings, clearing land for planting, and fighting off hostile natives fell to the laborers. Even the craftsmen among the company were not suited to clearing a wilderness and establishing a home. As a result, famine and starvation set in. At the end of that first winter, only 60 of the original settlers were still alive (Anderton 75). In 1609, the survivors actually decided to abandon their settlement and return to England. ("Colonial Library" 202). Although the plantation did not dissolve, it was such a commercial failure that, in 1624, after innumerable attempts to make the settlement economically independent, James I revoked the Virginia Company's charter and Jamestown came under the direct control of the Crown (Goddard 337).

Almost from the very beginning, the Jamestown Plantation survived only with outside help. As soon as the crude fort was completed in June 1607, Christopher Newport, captain of the *Susan Constant*, [***Now we are in Roman Numeral IV of Ella's preliminary outline.***] one of the three original ships, sailed for England. He returned to Jamestown in January 1608 with seventy additional settlers and supplies that were insufficient even for the men already living in the colony. Newport made a second voyage, again bringing back additional settlers and insufficient supplies. Still, the colonists, unable to grow and hunt their own food, and unable to find anything of commercial value to trade, grew dependent on the "supply missions."

It wasn't until 1610, with the arrival of the tobacco entrepreneur John Rolfe, that the settlement slowly became a profitable **[*Notice that, in the past few paragraphs, Ella has grown a little careless with her citation and documentation. She will need to fix this in her revision.*]** venture. While the Indians had shown the settlers how to grow the strain of tobacco familiar to them, Rolfe somehow managed to import seeds of the milder and sweeter tobacco grown in the southern Spanish colonies. Eventually, tobacco markets in Europe were clamoring for Virginia tobacco, and the Jamestown Plantation finally became a profitable enterprise. At the same time, a shift in the minds of the settlers was beginning to occur.

The Virginia Company had established Jamestown as a "plantation," a settlement established for the benefit of its investors. They had imposed unrealistic expectations on the tiny band of settlers: find gold where there were *rumors* of gold but no *evidence* of gold—later they added silver to the list, find a water route to Asia on a continent that would prove to be 3,000 miles across, and find the Lost Colony of Roanoke when no one was even certain where the original colony had been! While the settlers struggled just to stay alive, the Company kept sending more and more settlers and insufficient supplies. When Rolfe introduced his strain of tobacco, the settlers changed their mindset from working for the benefit of the Company to working toward their own benefit. The socialist/communist economy of the plantation slowly evolved into a private capital economy. The "plantation" was becoming a "colony" (Goddard 77).

Although James's revoking the Virginia Company's charter was still more than a decade away, already the Crown had learned some important lessons about establishing and governing new settlements in America. **[*We are now in Roman Numeral V of Ella's preliminary outline.*]** First, new settlements would be established as colonies—for the benefit of the settlers—not plantations—for the benefit of outside investors. Second, persons allowed to emigrate would have to have a strong reason for wanting to leave. The Puritan Separatists who sailed to America in 1620, for example, desired to establish a colony where they could worship as they saw fit without harassment from the government or society at large. Later colonies were established as refuges for debtors and other social misfits.

They also learned that, for colonies to be successful in the long term, women and families had to be allowed to travel with men. This would allow for a stability of life from the very beginning. Finally, they learned that colonies needed to be autonomous, self-governing and self-sustaining. If colonists had to borrow money for their passage, certainly they would be required to repay their debt, but colonies were no longer allowed to be completely financed by outside investors (Gallant 55—72).

Following England's disastrous early attempts to carve out a foothold in the Americas, and then the near-failure of the Jamestown Plantation, the English learned a few very important lessons that changed the nature of all future English colonies and actually pointed to the formation of the United States of America. *[This single sentence is Ella's first-draft conclusion.]*

What has Ella done right in this draft?

What does Ella need to improve when she revises?

THE HOME STRETCH

29. What am I aiming for now?

The final draft is *it*. It is the finished product. It is what you are giving your instructor for a grade. If you were a professional writer, the final draft is what you would be sending to your agent or editor for publication. It's what your reader is going to read.

Every aspect of your paper has to be working in this final draft.

> Your research is complete and as flawless as you can make it. (Perhaps writing and rereading your first draft showed you holes or imbalances in your information. They need to be fixed now.)

> Your organizational plan is logical and perfectly executed. (Again, throughout your research, you may have adapted your preliminary outline, adding where you encountered important aspects of your topic you hadn't thought of at first and deleting issues you thought you'd discuss but decided wouldn't work.)

> Your writing is correct, understandable, and interesting. (In your push to get your ideas on paper while writing your first draft, you may have composed some awkward sentences. You may have used a less clear or accurate word because you were unable to think of a better one. All of this needs to be fixed now.)

> Your format is absolutely as the instructor assigned it. (While composing your first draft, you were focusing on creating the "stuff" of your paper. That being done, now you need to pay attention to mundane details like where your instructor wants information like your name, course name, date of submission, etc. Your typed paper probably needs to be double-spaced. You were probably given guidelines about margins, indentations, etc. All of that needs to be taken care of now.)

In short, you are now searching for perfection. All of the individual parts of that perfection have been focused on and polished individually. Now, you simply need to put them all together.

The exceptions might be schools in which your instructor keeps returning drafts to you for revision until they are absolutely perfect. On the one hand, you hope that *each* draft will be your final draft, but your paper might actually go through three, four, or more drafts before it is accepted for grading.

30. Why, when, and how do I cite my sources?

Two issues we've already dealt with at some length are the issues of credibility and plagiarism. When we first talked about credibility, it was from the standpoint of your finding and using credible sources. Now that you are writing your final paper, you need to worry about your own credibility. Appropriate attribution and citation within your paper and documentation at the end of your paper will do a lot to bolster your credibility.

Likewise, being sincere and honest with where you got the facts, examples, and illustrations you are presenting—giving credit where credit is due—will greatly lessen the chances that someone—especially a slighted source—will charge you with taking credit for work that is not your own.

Imagine this: you tell a very funny joke to a friend. A little while later, you walk into a room and hear your friend tell *your* joke as if it were *his*. He gets the credit for making his audience laugh. At the very least, you would have expected your friend to say: "I heard the funniest joke from [insert your name here]" before telling the joke.

That's essentially what citation and documentation are: giving credit to the sources from which you got information for your paper.

One of the most basic forms of "giving credit" is the Works Cited Page at the end of your paper. Understand that this is a *requirement* of a research paper, not an option. You should *never* ask your teacher or professor whether a Works Cited Page is required because one is *always* required. *Every time* you consult a source that is outside of your own body of knowledge, you **must** include a Works Cited Page at the end of your paper—**even if it is not, strictly speaking, a research paper.**

> *NOTE:* The title of the page is *Works Cited*, which implies that you include only those works for which you have an in-text citation. The issue then becomes: if you *consulted* a source, got information or ideas from it, and *presented* information from that source in your paper, you need to cite that source, and it also needs to appear on your Works Cited Page.

The format of this page will be determined by your instructor, your school, or the field of study in which you have done your research. In your English classes, foreign language classes, and most other humanities classes, you will use the format prescribed by the Modern Language Association (MLA).

Generally, the Works Cited Page provides your reader with the author, title, publication data, and copyright date of the sources from which you took information in the creation of your own work. It will be in alphabetical order, based on the first letter of the entry (usually the author's or editor's last name).

A Works Cited entry for a book would look like this:

Last Name, First Name. <u>Title of Book.</u> City: Publishing Company, copyright.

Here's how Ella applies the template to her own sources:

Abnigail, Frances. <u>Black, White, and Red: Racial Conflict in America's First Colony.</u> Newark, NJ: Seminole Publishers, 1996.

Anderton, R. Keltho, ed. <u>Jamestown: Four Centuries of History.</u> Norfolk, VA: Patriot Press, 2007.

Gallant, Edward J. <u>Colonial Jamestown: A History for Young Readers.</u> New York: Seagull Group, 2000.

Goddard, Woodward, Ph. D. <u>Economics of Early North American Settlements.</u> Princeton, NJ: Princeton University Press, 2005.

Pollock, Benjamin. <u>Dictionary of American Historical Biography, Vol 1: 1600-1700.</u> New York: Lerner's Media, 1988.

<u>The Life of John Smith.</u> Los Angeles: POD Press, 1978.

Ella cannot find an author listed anywhere this book is advertised or reviewed. To find the author, she will have to look at the book itself—but only if she actually uses it for information. At this point, an anonymous book by a print-on-demand press is probably pretty low on her priority list.

A Works Cited entry for a magazine or newspaper article would look like this:

> Last, First. "Title of Article" Name of Newspaper or Magazine date of issue (European style): page number.

Here are two potential sources Ella's friend has just recommended to her:

> MacMahon, Willis. "Colonial America Before Slavery" <u>American Journal of Human Rights</u> July–August 2005: 95.

> "Jamestown Original Fort Discovered!" <u>New York Times Historical Digest</u> 1 April 2003: C-25.

A Works Cited entry for a website would look like this:

> <u>Title of Article or Website.</u> Author or producer of web information, copyright. <Universal Resource Locator (URL)>. Date accessed.

Ella has many websites and pages to document:

> <u>Colonists and Native Americans.</u> 01 June 1998. A part of the Texts and Documents project at Hanover College. 15 May 2008 <http://history.hanover.edu/project.html#17>.

Jamestown Settlement, living-history museum of early America.
22 January 2000. Jamestown-Yorktown Foundation, an agency
of the Commonwealth of Virginia that is accredited by the
American Association of Museums. 05 May 2008 <http://www.
historyisfun.org/Jamestown-Settlement.htm>.

The Virtual Jamestown Archive. 15 December 2001. Virginia
Polytechnic Institute and State University, the University of
Virginia, and the Virginia Center for Digital History. 15 May 2008
<http://www.virtualjamestown.org>.

Seekers of Truth in History. 01 April 1984. Americans for Truth,
Justice, and the American Way. 05 May 2008 <http://www.
truthhistory.org>.

"The Colonial Library." A Compendium of Primary Source
Documents. 08 August 2007. Dr. Richard Gander. 30 April 2008
<http://home.wi.rr.com/rickgander/primarysources.htm>.

The United States and Moral Compromise. 23 March 2001. No
affiliated organization or institution cited. 41 April 2008 <http://
www.morallycompromised.com>.

Works Cited entries for several miscellaneous types of sources are
shown below. While Ella may or may not end up using any of these types of
sources, Rob has:

An Article in a Web Magazine

Author(s). "Title of Article." Title of Online Publication. Date of Publication. Date of
Access <electronic address>.

A Personal Interview (Listed by the name of the person interviewed):

Last, First. Personal Interview. Date of interview (European style).

A Lecture or Speech

> Speaker's Last Name, First Name. "Title of Speech: How was it presented in the event's program." Full location of delivery (Heimholtz Gymnasium, University of Southern Norton, Mewaukins, CT.) Date (European style).

If there is no title, label the speech according to its type (e.g., Guest Lecture, Keynote Address, State of the Union Address, etc.).

A Painting, Sculpture, or Photograph

> Artist's Last Name, First. Title of Work. Year Created. Building where work is on display, City.

If you're citing a photograph of a work, include all of the above information, as well as the bibliographic information for the source in which the photograph appears:

> Artist's Last Name, First. Title of Work. Year Created. Building where work is on display, City. Title of Book or Magazine Where You Saw Photograph. By Author's name (First and Last). City: Publisher, copyright. Page or plate number.

Broadcast Television or Radio Program

> "Title of Episode." Name of Series. Network. Call letters of local affiliate on which you viewed the program, City. Date of broadcast (European style).

Recorded Television Shows

> "Title of Episode." Name of Series. Writ. Names of writers (First and Last). Dir. Name of Director (First and Last). Network of Original Broadcast. Date of Original Broadcast. Format (VHS, DVD, etc.). Producer of Recording, copyright of recording.

Movies in Theaters

Title of Movie. Dir. Name of Director (First and Last). Perf. Names of Key Performers (First and Last, separated by commas). Production company, copyright.

Recorded Movies

Title of Movie. Dir. Name of Director (First and Last). Perf. Names of Performers (First and Last, separated by commas). Copyright date of movie. Format (VHS, DVD, etc.). Production company of recording, Copyright date of recording.

NOTE 1: Every detail of the above formats is important to copy in your material. Where the sample has a period, you must place a period. Where the sample has a comma, you must place a comma, etc.

NOTE 2: While many printers and designers advise that underlining is stylistically bad (in print, underlining is a code for *italics*), the *MLA Handbook* recommends underlining material that is italicized in print.

NOTE 3: Because there are so many variations on the above types of sources, especially websites and electronic sources, it is virtually impossible to "learn" every form. In addition, the forms are revised frequently. Rather than spend your time trying to memorize the format for each type of entry, find a good style sheet or handbook that provides examples of each type of source and learn how to follow it.

EXERCISE ONE:

ANALYZING THE REQUIREMENTS OF THE WORKS CITED PAGE

Examine all of the previous templates and models and explain what they have in common. What basic guideline can you infer about formatting entries on your Works Cited Page?

When is the author's or artist's name presented last name first?

EXERCISE TWO:

PRACTICING THE WORKS CITED PAGE FORMAT

Now, help Rob format his sources for his Works Cited Pages:

Rob

1. http://www.npr.org/klbj/exam/rbeature/rb_interview.html
    National Public Radio Broadcast: "From Sea to Shining Sea,
    the History of Transcontinental Travel." On a weekly program
    called *Experiencing America*, commentator, Jenkins, F. Lloyd.
    This episode aired in the morning of May 2, 2008.

    "From Sea to Shining Sea, the History of Transcontinental Travel."
    Experiencing America. Comment. F. Lloyd Jenkins. NPR.
    WMMR, Dayton. 2 Feb. 2008.

2. Website: http://cprr.org/Museum/Chinese.html— "A Tribute to
    the Contributions of Chinese-American to the First North
    American Transcontinental Railroad," a part of the First
    North American Transcontinental Railroad Photographic
    Virtual Museum. Last updated: January 17, 2003. I visited the
    site on April 18, 2008.

    A Tribute to the Contributions of Chinese-American to the First
    North American Transcontinental Railroad. 17 January
    2003. First North American Transcontinental Railroad
    Photographic Virtual Museum. 18 April 2008 <http://cprr.
    org/Museum/Chinese.html.>

3. *The Tenuous Relationship between the Government of the United States of
    America and the Railroads of the Pacific States*, by Victor H. Poole
    1871—Greene and Greyhound, New York.

    Poole, Victor H. The Tenuous Relationship between the Government
    of the United States of America and the Railroads of the
    Pacific States. New York: Greene and Greyhound, 1871.

4.   Article from the May 26, 2008 *Weekly News of the World*—"Golden
        Spike Found! Heiress Turns Historical Object into Bracelet."
        (Begins on page 17.)

"Golden Spike Found! Heiress Turns Historical Object into Bracelet."
    <u>Weekly News of the World</u>. 26 May 2008: 17.

EXERCISE THREE:

WRITING YOUR OWN WORKS CITED PAGE

Now, apply what you've learned and practiced and write the Works Cited
entries for your own sources.

In addition to the Works Cited Page, whenever you refer to one of your
sources in the text of your paper, you must provide an in-text or parenthetical
citation. This is, quite simply, a brief mention of the source—usually the author's
last name or an abbreviated form of the title—and the page number (if there is
one) in parentheses at the end of the material derived from the source:

(Pearson 87)
(Conchina 34)
(Dunnel C12)

If there is no stated author, then use an abbreviated form of the title, along
with the page number:

("Slavery in Colonial Virginia" 35)

These are the basic forms for citing *all* information from your sources,
whether it is in the form of a direct quotation, paraphrase, or summary. If
you must provide a parenthetical citation for every quotation, paraphrase, or
summary of a source, you might wonder: *doesn't that mean that everything in my
paper will be cited and documented?*

The answer, of course, is that it does not. You've taken notes that contain your own thoughts, ideas, and insights, as well as information from your sources. In Ella's and Rob's first drafts you've seen how well (or how badly) they present their ideas and incorporate their interpretations, evaluations, and insights. These, of course, are not documented because there is no source to document. As you examine the first draft of your paper and prepare the final draft, if you find yourself citing and documenting every sentence, every paragraph, every bit of information and insight you present, then you know that you have not contributed enough to the discussion. What you would be writing would be a research report, not a thesis-driven research paper.

Important Variation 1: If you attribute a quotation or paraphrase to the source in the body of your paper, then you omit the author's name from the material in the parentheses.

For example:

(No attribution in the text):

Some historians still cling to the delusion that the African slave trade was not as horrendous as anti-slavers would have us believe: "When a man is taken from the savage jungle and placed in the safety of a southern plantation where he will have steady employment, where is the harm?" (Fulton 293).

(Attribution in the text—direct quotation):

Some historians still cling to the delusion that the African slave trade was not as horrendous as anti-slavers would have us believe. As Roberta Fulton notes, "When a man is taken from the savage jungle and placed in the safety of a southern plantation where he will have steady employment, where is the harm?" (293).

(Attribution in the text—paraphrase):

Some historians still cling to the delusion that the African slave trade was not as horrendous as anti-slavers would have us believe. Roberta Fulton suggests that the relative safety of the plantation was such a gain for the enslaved that his lack of liberty was a small price to pay (293).

Important Variation 2: If you have more than one source by the same author on your Works Cited Page, include an abbreviated version of the title of the source you are citing in the parentheses.

For example:

(No attribution in the text):

Some historians still cling to the delusion that the African slave trade was not as horrendous as anti-slavers would have us believe: "When a man is taken from the savage jungle and placed in the safety of a southern plantation where he will have steady employment, where is the harm?" (Fulton, The Optimist's Guide to Slavery 293).

(Attribution in the text—direct quotation):

Some historians still cling to the delusion that the African slave trade was not as horrendous as anti-slavers would have us believe. Roberta Fulton notes "When a man is taken from the savage jungle and placed in the safety of a southern plantation where he will have steady employment, where is the harm?" (The Optimist's Guide to Slavery 293).

(Attribution in the text—paraphrase):

Some historians still cling to the delusion that the African slave trade was not as horrendous as anti-slavers would have us believe. Roberta Fulton suggests that the relative safety of the plantation was such a gain for the enslaved that his lack of liberty was a small price to pay (The Optimist's Guide to Slavery 293).

Important Variation 3: If you choose to mention the title of the source in the body of the paragraph, then you do not need to repeat that information in the parentheses.

For example: Some historians still cling to the delusion that the African slave trade was not as horrendous as anti-slavers would have us believe. Roberta Fulton notes in <u>The Optimist's Guide to Slavery,</u> her questionable study of the beginnings of the Atlantic slave trade: "When a man is taken from the savage jungle and placed in the safety of a southern plantation where he will have steady employment, where is the harm?" (293).

If you consider the logic, handling these scenarios should be fairly easy, as should any new ones you encounter. Attribution, citation, and documentation formats are based on the principles of giving your reader all of the information he or she might need to locate the source and verify the accuracy of the information, while at the same time, saving you from having to repeat author, title, and other publication data.

31. How do I make absolutely certain I am protected against charges of plagiarism?

If you have carefully followed our instructions and advice from the beginning, there is virtually no chance that you will be accused of plagiarism.

Once again, however,

> as you write your paper (especially if you compose at the keyboard), and revise your draft(s), *do not* merely cut and paste *even so much as one word* from another source;

> make it a point to *attribute all quotations* in the body of your paper;

> *disclose the source* of key information or viewpoints in the body of your paper;

> *develop and share your own ideas and insights*, as well as present the information you've gathered.

In addition:

> do not panic and resort to an online paper mill or some other paper writing service;

> do not persuade a parent, friend, or sibling to "help" you write your paper;

> study your notes and review your material enough so that you can answer questions about your topic, your sources, and the process you used in researching and writing this paper.

In short, by this point you know what plagiarism is and how to avoid it.

32. How do I edit my research paper?

The first part of this all-important editing step is to understand what you are to do. You have written the first *draft* of your paper. If you've done everything you needed to do in all of the previous steps, you should have a pretty good draft—that's why we're not calling it a "rough draft."

However, it is *not* ready to submit to your teacher for a grade. If you are like just about every professional writer and most good students, your draft will need a good bit of polish. It might even need some structural help. In some rare cases, it might need to be tossed aside so you can start again.

Do a quick Internet search for "Editing Services" and look at the range of services available and how much each costs. *We are not recommending that you employ any of these for your paper!* First of all, at this point in your education, to hire an editing service would most likely constitute cheating, with penalties potentially as severe as for plagiarism. Second, for every truly legitimate editing service that advertises on the Internet, there are probably two or three scams that will take your money and circle a few misspelled words and maybe indicate a missing comma or two in return.

What the array of editing services and their range of services should show you is that this step in producing your paper is much, much more than merely proofreading for spelling and punctuation.

Here are the degrees of editing you should be prepared to do:

> **General overview:** Overall, how does the paper read?

Are the tone and voice appropriate—not too informal, but not too "stuffy"?

Is it interesting?

Are the logic and the progression of ideas clear?

Are all of your points sufficiently discussed with support from your sources?

Is every piece of information (including quotations, paraphrases, summaries, and key facts and concepts) from a source cited and documented appropriately, with the appropriate attribution?

In short, does the paper do what it sets out to do? Does it meet the needs of the original assignment?

> **Content edit**: How convincing, accurate, and thorough is your argument?

Does your introduction clearly state your thesis and provide an overview of the arguments you are going to make?

Does your conclusion bring your paper back to your thesis?

Is each sub-point argued and developed adequately?

Is there an appropriate balance between evidence from your sources and your own insight and discussion?

Is each individual paragraph adequate? Does each paragraph contribute to your argument? Have you avoided all tangents? Are there any holes in your logic or evidence?

Do you provide sufficient background information that your reader might need in order to understand your point?

> *NOTE:* It is common in this stage to eliminate paragraphs that do not add anything to the paper, compose new paragraphs that contain information that seems missing, or rearrange paragraphs to better communicate with your reader.

> **Fact check**: At some point before you turn in your final paper, you're going to have to make certain that:

(1) your sources have given you accurate information, and that

(2) you have recorded and reported that information accurately.

If you are found to be misrepresenting facts—and it's not hard for a teacher who knows the subject matter to recognize factual errors—you will probably receive a failing grade for your paper. *You cannot defend yourself by blaming your source(s) if you misrepresent what they say.*

> **Source Check**: Make certain you've attributed the right information to the right sources and that every bit of information that is not your original thought is credited to its source(s). In addition, make certain you have *every detail* of your source listed correctly:

(1) authors' names presented accurately and spelled correctly,

(2) full and complete title(s),

(3) correct dates, volume number, page numbers, URLs, etc.,

> **Line Edit**: Check *each sentence* for problems in grammar, syntax, sentence structure, mechanics, etc. Check *each word* to make certain it is the best, clearest, and most appropriate word you can use to communicate your idea.

> **Proofreading**: We're *editing* right now. You will proofread before you submit your final draft.

The important thing to remember in this step is that a draft is much, much more than a copy. This step is your chance to perfect your paper.

Here are Ella's revisions to parts of her first draft. We've underlined the new material Ella has added and drew a line through material Ella has decided to cut. We've also provided examples of Ella's thinking in making the changes that she's made.

Example 1:

<u>Nobel-Prize-winning economist Woodward Goddard explains the structure of the corporation chartered by the Crown with the express purpose of colonizing the New World.</u> [*Ella is going to be more transparent about her sources and their credibility. This will make her own arguments stronger.*] The branch of the Virginia Company that established Jamestown was called The London Company ~~(Goddard 73)~~. [*Since this entire section of information comes from the same source (Goddard), Ella needs to cite the source only at the end.*] A rival branch, the Plymouth Company, was established at the same time but never fulfilled its charter ~~(Goddard 73)~~. <u>As the company's purpose was to generate a profit for the royal treasury, the first settlement was planned with three essential goals: find gold, find a viable trade route to Asia, and find the Lost Colony of Roanoke (73-77).</u> [*Ella introduced Goddard at the beginning of this paragraph, so she does not need to repeat his name in her parenthetical citation.*] ~~The first Jamestown settlers sailed in three ships, leaving England in December 1606. James I assigned them three goals: find gold, find a viable trade route to Asia, and find the Lost Colony of Roanoke. ("Colonial Library" 275).~~ [*The dates and the fact that they sailed in the three ships are essentially irrelevant to Ella's argument. She wants to stay within the 6-10 page assignment, so she knows she needs to cut some non-essential material to make room for more important information.*]

<u>These unrealistic goals, according to letters from John Smith and Christopher Newport, who captained one of the three ships of the original passage, challenged the mission from the very beginning.</u> ~~Already the mission was challenged, not only because of the bad weather that delayed the voyage, but~~

because None of the reasons for the settlement was of importance ~~to very few~~ most of the settlers. Most were, essentially, little more than underpaid employees of the Virginia Company.

Example 2:

This first band of settlers was also poorly suited for carving a new civilization out of a strange and uninhabitable wilderness. ~~In May 1607, when they finally reached land, in the territory they were calling Virginia,~~ Even Captain Smith recorded his dissatisfaction with the "personnel" sent by the Virginia Company to seek their fortunes in the New World: "Wythe so menny Gentylmenne amoungst our companye, howe are we to survive? Will the Gentylmen cut trees and hew lumbre? Will they plow land [*This direct quotation from a primary source helps Ella establish the validity of her point that the settlers of Jamestown were not suited to the task to which they had been assigned.*] and plant croppes? And the precious Craftsmen, whose hands cannot be sullied with mere physical labour, are of little use as welle"("Colonial Library" 103).

They chose to settle on an island about 40 miles inland from where the Atlantic Ocean ~~ends and the~~ meets the Chesapeake Bay. They called the river the James River (~~after King James~~) and chose the spot because they thought ~~the land~~ it would be easy to defend ~~if they were attacked by sea by a European power like France or Spain~~ against attack(~~"Jamestown Fort Discovered" C-27~~). [*Again, because Ella is adding some important information, she must cut some words to maintain her page length.*] They also thought the plentiful water would make farming easier ("Jamestown Fort Discovered" C-27).

In both of the previous examples, notice that Ella is doing far more than merely correcting spelling and punctuation or changing an occasional word. She is making some fairly extensive cuts, evaluating her material, and deciding that some of it is irrelevant. She is adding some direct discussion of her sources, revealing to her reader where she learned the information she is passing on. Additionally, she is adding some essential information, especially in the form of direct quotations, that will make her argument stronger and clearer.

EXERCISE FOUR:

EVALUATING STUDENT REVISIONS

Here is Rob's revision for the excerpt from the first draft we checked for potential plagiarism in Chapter 5. Examine the changes he has made and then answer the questions that follow.

Rob

First Draft:

"The idea of securing Chinese arose because they had already helped build the California Central Railroad that ran from Sacramento to Marysville. The Chinese had also built the San Jose Railway. Critics of the idea originally thought the diminutive Chinese were too small to tackle such a momentous task. Charles Crocker of Central Pacific pointed out, however, that 'the Chinese made the Great Wall, didn't they?'"

"The first Chinese were hired in 1865 for approximately $28 per month. Their assignment was to do the very dangerous work of blasting, and laying ties over the treacherous terrain of the high Sierras. These noble and hardworking 'foreigners' lived in simple huts and cooked their own meals of fish, dried oysters and fruit, mushrooms and seaweed."

"The work was difficult and progressed slowly; the terrain on which they were laying track rose 7,000 feet in 100 miles. To conquer the many nearly perpendicular slopes, workers used techniques they had learned in China. They were lowered by ropes from the top of cliffs in baskets. While hanging there, they chipped away at the granite and planted explosives."

Revision:

Morrison credits Charles Crocker of the Central Pacific Railroad with first noticing that the Chinese had already helped build the California Central and the San Jose Railways. When it was suggested to him that the Chinese might be too small of stature to perform such arduous labor, he replied, "the Chinese made the Great Wall, didn't they?" (Railroadhistory. org). So respected were these men for their dedication and ingenuity that, when they were first hired in 1865, they were paid approximately $28 per month (Railroadhistory.org), which was significantly higher than the $20 per month the Irish were paid (Grandolf 78). Moreover, the Chinese were allowed to live quietly in their own camp and cook and eat food more to their liking (*Asians and the Great Railroad*). While Morrison would like to see racism in this segregation of the Chinese, Grandolf sees the desire to be respectful to a minority culture.

There is no doubt that the work performed by these men was extremely dangerous and grueling. Geological Historian Maureen Dodd explains that the rock was solid granite, and the slope of the mountains on which the Chinese were supposed to lay track was often as much as a 7,000-foot rise in 100 feet (116). With nowhere to stand, the men allowed themselves to be suspended in baskets, from which they chipped into the rock and planted their explosives (122).

What were some of Rob's original problems?

Has he overcome them?

Why or why not?

33. What does a completed look like?

You've been following Ella's progress pretty closely from the initial assignment of her research paper until now, her due date. Here is the final paper that she turned in to her teacher:

Ella Anonym   1

US History 11

Ms. Breddin-Bodder

12 May 2008

The Lessons of Jamestown

With Christopher Columbus's discovery of what the Europeans called the "New World," a mad scramble began to colonize the land and exploit its vast natural resources. Spain, the most powerful nation in the world, had already established several successful colonies, as had France. England, however, anxious to take its place as a world power beside its two neighbors—and enemies—had not yet succeeded. Sir Walter Raleigh's Roanoke had failed, and Queen Elizabeth died without having established her foothold in North America.

James I, however, refused to merely watch while his rivals built empires. He demanded an American colony, and chartered The Virginia Company, the corporation that would eventually give him

---

the Jamestown Plantation. This poorly planned and badly staffed commercial venture nearly failed a number of times, but the lessons learned through these difficulties helped shape the nature of future British settlements in America and the nature of the future United States itself.

What the British learned from their frustrations with Jamestown was that the settlers had to have a vested interest in the colony's success. People fleeing some sort of persecution or freeing themselves from debt or just seeking a new start would fight for the success of their settlement more fiercely than mere employees or servants would. These settlers would also have to be able to demonstrate that they had a knowledge or skill that would contribute to the *establishment* of a settlement—often skills very different from those most valued in an already-thriving civilization. The would-be colonizers also learned that, if they were going to establish a lasting presence in the new land, the settlers would need to be allowed to build new lives. They would need *all* of the necessities—including the companionship of women. The frequent and nearly disastrous conflicts with the native Algonquins taught the British important lessons about relations with the aboriginal inhabitants. Finally, they learned that a successful colony was an autonomous and independent society, self-governing and self-sustaining; and therein lay the seeds of United States independence.

James I's goals—thoroughly mercenary—were shortsighted at best and ill advised at worst. Because his one desire for New World exploration was to enrich the royal coffers, his approach to colonization was typically corporate. Rather than establishing the seventeenth-century equivalent of a cabinet agency to oversee expanding British culture to the New World, James chartered a corporation. Nobel-Prize-winning economist Woodward Goddard explains the two-branch structure of the Virginia Company. The branch that established Jamestown was called The London Company. The rival branch, the Plymouth Company, was established at the same time, but never fulfilled its charter. As the company's purpose was to generate a profit for the royal treasury, the first settlement was planned with three essential goals: find gold, find a viable trade route to Asia, and find the Lost Colony of Roanoke (73-77).

These unrealistic goals, according to letters from John Smith and Christopher Newport, who captained one of the three ships of the original passage, set the mission up for failure from the very beginning. None of the reasons for the settlement was important to the settlers, most of whom were little more than underpaid employees of the Virginia Company. The investors, who had the most to gain from the venture's success, had stayed safely in London ("Colonial Library" 98). By the same token, the settlers—even the ones who expected to make their own fortunes, as well as the fortunes of their investors—probably cared very little about James's desire for an empire and for a full royal treasury. Had more of the settlers had a personal interest in the success of their settlement, they might have worked, if not harder, certainly smarter.

Rolls of the original 105 settlers show that the passengers of those first three ships included six members of the Council, one member of the clergy, 49 "gentlemen," 13 laborers (including 1 surgeon), and four boys (Virtual Jamestown). The rest were craftsmen: a tailor, a bricklayer, a barber, etc. (Virtual Jamestown). What each man's—there were no

Anonym   5

women on this first voyage—reason for wanting to come to America may have been is not known. Some were probably seeking adventure. Some were probably hoping to start a new life. For all of them, their personal reasons for the venture were largely overlooked, certainly not recorded by history, in favor of the commercial goals of finding gold and a trade route to Asia.

This first band of settlers was also poorly suited for carving a new civilization out of a strange and uninhabitable wilderness. Even Captain Smith recorded his dissatisfaction with the "personnel" sent by the Virginia Company to seek their fortunes in the New World:

> Wythe so menny Gentylmenne amoungst our companye, howe are we to survive? Will the Gentylmen cut trees and hew lumbre? Will they plow land and plant croppes? And the precious Craftsmen, whose hands cannot be sullied with mere physical labour, are of little use as welle. ("Colonial Library" 103)

They chose an island as their permanent landing spot, about 40 miles upriver from the mouth of the Chesapeake Bay. The spot seemed easy to defend, and the leaders thought the plentiful water would make farming easier ("Jamestown Fort Discovered" C-27).

But they were mistaken. Smith himself recorded in his 12 June 1609 entry:

> Thysse infernal soil doth produce nought but biting insekts and bleeding blisters. The seed is no sooner playnted than it is swallowed by the capacious jaws of the swamp. If any plant doth indeed take root, it is quickly o'erpowered by the lustier vegetation of the jungle. There is nought wholesom to be had in all this island. ("Colonial Library" 97)

Anonym   6

Not only was there "nought wholesom" on the island, but the river itself was salt water and tidal, affecting the availability of drinking water and the ability to flee should the occasion call for it. The surrounding area was also inhabited by Indians, who attacked almost immediately and proved to be on-again-off-again enemies to the settlers throughout Jamestown's existence ("Jamestown Fort Discovered" C-27). Marshy land led to crop failures. The island's isolation meant that it lacked the large game animals that would be needed to feed the entire population. The "gentlemen," as Smith had predicted, refused to work, and the tasks of building a fort, storehouse, church, and dwellings, clearing land for planting, and fighting off hostile natives fell to the laborers. Even the craftsmen among the company were not suited to clearing a wilderness and establishing homes. As a result, famine and starvation set in. At the end of that first winter, only 60 of the original settlers were still alive (Anderton 75). In 1609, the survivors actually decided to abandon their settlement and return to England ("Colonial Library" 202). Although the plantation did not dissolve, it remained such a commercial failure that, in 1624, after innumerable attempts to make the settlement economically independent, James I revoked the Virginia Company's charter, and Jamestown came under the direct control of the Crown (Goddard 337).

Almost from the very beginning, the Jamestown Plantation survived only with outside help. As soon as the crude fort was completed in June 1607, Christopher Newport, captain of the *Susan Constant,* one of the three original ships, sailed for England. He returned to Jamestown in January 1608 with seventy additional settlers and supplies that all sources agree were insufficient even for the men already living in the colony. Newport made a second voyage, again bringing back additional settlers and insufficient supplies. Still, the colonists, unable to grow and hunt their own food, and unable to find anything of commercial value to trade, grew dependent on the "supply missions."

It wasn't until 1610, with the arrival of the tobacco entrepreneur John Rolfe, that the settlement slowly became a profitable venture. While the natives had shown the settlers how to grow the strain of tobacco familiar to them, Rolfe somehow managed to import seeds of the milder and sweeter tobacco grown in the southern Spanish colonies. Eventually, tobacco markets in Europe were clamoring for Virginia tobacco, and the Jamestown Plantation finally became a profitable enterprise. At the same time, a shift in the minds of the settlers was beginning to occur.

As Goddard explains, the Virginia Company had established Jamestown as a "plantation," a settlement established for the benefit of its investors (200). Historian Keltho Anderton emphasizes the unrealistic expectations the Company had imposed on the tiny band of settlers: find gold where there were *rumors* of gold but no *evidence* of gold—later they added silver to the list—, find a water route to Asia on a continent that would prove to be 3,000 miles across, and find the Lost Colony of Roanoke when no one was even certain where the original colony had been! (126). While the settlers struggled just to stay alive, the Company kept sending more and more settlers and insufficient supplies. Rolfe's introduction of his strain of tobacco prompted the settlers to change their priorities. Where they had previously been working for the benefit of the Company, now they were working for their own benefit. What Goddard describes as the socialist/communist economy of the plantation slowly evolved into a private capital economy. The "plantation" was becoming a "colony" (77).

Although it would still be more than a decade before James would revoke the Virginia Company's charter, already the Crown had learned some important lessons about how it would establish and govern its American empire. First, new settlements would be established as colonies—for the benefit of the settlers— not plantations—for the benefit of outside investors (Anderton 437). Second, persons allowed to emigrate would have to have a strong reason for wanting to leave. The Puritan Separatists who sailed to America in 1620, for example, desired to establish a colony where they could worship as they saw fit without harassment from the government or society at large. Later colonies were established as refuges for debtors and other social misfits.

James also learned that, for colonies to be successful in the long term, women and families had to be allowed to travel with men. This would allow for a stability of life from the very beginning. Interestingly, this is the point most emphasized by Edward Gallant in his "young readers" history. Finally, the king learned that colonies needed to be autonomous, self-governing, and self-sustaining. If colonists had to borrow money for their passage, they would certainly be required to repay their debt, but colonies were no longer allowed to be completely financed by outside investors (Gallant 55-72).

The rest is, as they say, history. The Massachusetts colony—and through Massachusetts, Rhode Island and Connecticut—the Georgia colony, and the Pennsylvania colony all followed. Each was successful, and the British presence grew in America until England controlled thirteen colonies spanning the full east coast of what is now the United States. The lessons James and his successors learned fighting to keep the struggling Jamestown alive proved invaluable in facilitating the success of the later colonies. Ironically, however, those same lessons—especially regarding a colony's autonomy and self-sufficiency—paved the way for thirteen independent colonies to unite and assert their political independence from the nation that had originally given them life.

Works Cited

Anderton, R. Keltho, ed. <u>Jamestown: Four Centuries of History.</u> Norfolk, VA: Patriot Press, 2007.

Gallant, Edward J. <u>Colonial Jamestown: A History for Young Readers</u>. New York: Seagull Group, 2000.

Goddard, Woodward, Ph. D. <u>Economics of Early North American Settlements</u>. Princeton, NJ: Princeton University Press, 2005.

"Jamestown Original Fort Discovered!" <u>New York Times Historical Digest</u> 1 April 2003: C-25.

"The Colonial Library." <u>A Compendium of Primary Source Documents</u>. 08 August 2007. Dr. Richard Gander. <http://home.wi.rr.com/rickgander/ primarysources.htm> 30 April 2008.

<u>The Virtual Jamestown Archive</u>. 15 December 2001. Virginia Polytechnic Institute and State University, the University of Virginia, and the Virginia Center for Digital History. 22 April 2008 <http://www.virtualjamestown.org>.

34. How can I fix any careless errors that could lower my grade?

There's an adage that says, "The devil is in the details," and this is absolutely true in the worlds of academics and publishing. While the arrival of the personal computer and word-processing program made the processes of revision and proofreading easier than they had ever been before, it also raised the standard for final draft correctness. Whereas, in the days of the typewriter and carbon paper, a writer may actually have been allowed to submit a manuscript with one or two minor typographical errors per page, today, the entire manuscript is expected to be error-free. Since the technology exists to find an error and correct it without having to retype an entire page, the writer is expected to use it.

Therefore, your final draft needs to be as close to perfect as this paper is going to be, and you, the writer, have no excuse for flaws—especially easily correctable flaws—that will detract from the overall quality of your work. It is, therefore, in your best interest to take a day or two before your final paper is due and pay attention to the details.

Before you print:

1. **Run a spelling and grammar check.** *Do not allow any automatic changes or "change-alls."* You must look at each "error" your computer finds and each "correction" it suggests. Spelling and grammar checks do not recognize last names, place names, and variant or archaic spellings. Ella does not want to lose points because she followed her computer's advice when it told her to change *John Rolfe to John Rifle.*

2. **Scroll through every page of your paper and made certain everything is formatted the way you want it.** Word processing programs often do interesting things to blocks of text when you cut or copy from one document and paste into another. Margins and indentation; bolding or italics; even text size, font, and color can be change simply by pressing "delete" to make one paragraph merge with the paragraph above it.

3. **Reread your Works Cited Page** and make certain it is correct and that *you have followed your teacher's instructions to the letter* (for example, underlining where the instructions say to underline; p and pp for "page" and "pages;" periods, commas, and colons where the instructions say to place them).

4. **Read your entire paper one last time** to check for errors the spelling and grammar check might not have caught. "Two" is spelled correctly, but not if the word you want is "too." "Thin king" is spelled correctly, but does not mean the same thing as "thinking." *This is your final draft, submitted for a grade and/or publication. You teacher is absolutely justified in penalizing you for carelessness.*

5. **Double-check your document set-up.** Do your name and the page numbers appear where your instructions say they should? Were you instructed to have a title page? Is yours set up the way you were instructed? Make no mistake; research papers will receive lower grades simply on the basis of improper formatting.

Print a copy of your paper:

6. **Reread it one last time** for any errors or problems you may have missed when reading the paper on your monitor.

7. **Have one other trusted person read your paper,** just to look for any language or format problems you may have missed. *This is not an edit. You do not want content advice or suggestions for rewriting sentences, paragraphs, or sections of your paper.* But, if you have forgotten to put the parentheses around a citation, or if you've italicized the titles of books on your Works Cited Page instead of underlining them, you want this trusted person to tell you.

8. **Key all final corrections** into the document on your computer.

Print the final, clean copy of your paper:

9. **Submit your paper.**

10. **Wait for your A+.**

Chapter
8

EXTRAS

35. What other documentation formats are there?

In this book, we have modeled and used the Modern Language Association (MLA) format. This is the format you will use in your English (or any other world language) class, your art and music class, or any subject included in the arts and humanities. Another very common format—one you will almost certainly have to use at one time or another—is the American Psychological Association (APA) format. This is the form used in psychology and the social sciences, including history, geography, education, anthropology, etc.

As with MLA, there is little point trying to *learn* the style. The requirements do change from time to time, and it would be best for you simply to learn how to follow the model. As you look at the samples below, note where APA and MLA are similar, and where they are different.

The rule of documentation is the same. Every time you present someone else's work, whether you quote, paraphrase, or summarize, you must give credit.

In APA, however, that credit includes essentially the author's name and the copyright date:

> The institution of slavery dates as far back as recorded history (Baxten, 1994).

If you name the author in the text:

> According to Baxten (1994), the institution of slavery dates back as far as recorded history.

If you refer to an entire web site:

The website of the Human Rights Watchdogs of the Global Village provides up-to-date information on suspected cases of slavery in the modern world (http://www.humrigwatdog.org/).

To refer to a specific page or chapter:

Baxten (1994, p. 62) notes that "slaves were often the spoils of war, gifts from rival tribes suing for peace, even the children of wives who had fallen into disfavor." In the Christian New Testament, the Apostle Paul wrote his epistles to an audience that took the existence of slavery for granted, and Paul did not object to it (Mishigus & Molloy, 2002, chap. 5).

If there is no stated author, include the first 1-3 key words from the title:

"Slaves were often the spoils of war, gifts from rival tribes suing for peace, even the children of wives who had fallen into disfavor" ("History of Slavery," 2005, p. 20).

In the APA format, the "Works Cited Page" is called a "Reference List:"

The reference list includes all the sources mentioned in the body of your paper, arranged in alphabetical order by the authors' last names—or by the first word of the title if the author is not named.

The basic formats include (again, note where APA and MLA are similar and where they are different):

Books

Last name, Initials. (Publication year). Title of book. City and state where published: Name of publisher.

Periodicals

Last name, Initials. (Publication date). Title of article. Title of periodical, volume number, page numbers.

Online Sources

As you did in MLA, supply both the date the material was published and the date you retrieved it.

Note also the hanging indentation (similar to MLA).

If you cite more than one source by the same author, list them in order of their publication dates order, with *older before newer.* Include the author's name in both entries.

If the source lists six or fewer authors, supply the names and initials of all of them. If there are more than six authors, supply only the first six names followed by *"et al"* (Latin for "and others").

Sample Reference List

Carton, S. (2003, April 27). Spoils of war? *Historical Review,* 151. Retrieved May 21, 2008, from http://www.onlinejournal.com/HR/magazine/carton/spoils.html.

Evigans, G. (2001, October 15). Slavery and indentured servitude. *Historical Review,* 130, 22-23. Retrieved May 21, 2008, from http://www.onlinejournal.com/HR/magazine/evigans/slavery.html.

Goldberg, J.K. (2007, August 12). Neither slave nor free. *News of the World in Review,* 53, 61-62.

Grossman, T. and Canandagua, G. (2008, January 13). Born free. In T. Grossman (Producer), *The African-American Heritage.* Philadelphia: National Public Radio. Retrieved June 2, 2008, from eLibrary database.

Klepperer, R.P. (1999). Economics of slavery. In *Encyclopedia of Economics* (2nd ed.). (Vol. 3, pp. 82-91). NewYork: J. Wilbert & Sons.

Larkin, J. (1988). Slavery across cultures. *Journal of Cultural History,* 54(3), 18-24.

McMahon, W. & Matthews, P. (Eds.). (2004). On *The Shoulders of Slaves* (3rd ed.). New York: H. Lupinsky.

McMahon, W. & Matthews, P. (Eds.) (2007). *Slaves of our Fathers.* Cambridge, MA: Harvard University Press.

Schnaple, B. (2004, November 12). More evidence of pre–Columbian American slavery. *New York News Journal*, pp. A1, A14.

Seidley, B. (2005). *Slavery and the Cinderella Myth.* New York: Columbia University Center for Culture and History.

Shelley, L. (2008, April 13). *The Candidate's Slave-Owning Ancestors.* Retrieved June 2, 2008, from http://www.polwatch.wwn.net /news/ news 769413g.html.

U.S. Department of Delayed Justice. (2005). *Reparations to Descendents of American Slaves.* (NBS Publication 6). Washington, DC: Author.

Volezinger, J. (1999). Historical and economic justifications for slavery. In P.Q. Santos (Ed.), *The Rise and Fall of Mighty Civilizations.* (pp. 157-195). New York: Winston and Sons.

Whalley, P. (Producer). (2005). *From Cotton Field to Oval Office.* [DVD]. Los Angeles: MediaLeft.